The FINAL FAREWELL

by Ray Deaton

RoseDog Books

PITTSBURGH, PENNSYLVANIA 15238

The contents of this work including, but not limited to, the accuracy of events, people, and places depicted; opinions expressed; permission to use previously published materials included; and any advice given or actions advocated are solely the responsibility of the author, who assumes all liability for said work and indemnifies the publisher against any claims stemming from publication of the work.

RoseDog Books
585 Alpha Drive
Suite 103
Pittsburgh, PA 15238
Visit our website at www.rosedogbookstore.com

ISBN: 979-8-89127-762-5
eISBN: 979-8-89127-260-6

The FINAL FAREWELL

This dedicated to all those that had to say a final farewell to a loved one as the loved one departed this world for hopefully, a better world.

Although the title is *The Final Farewell*, it is, I believe, necessary to consider an equation, an equation for life, in order to understand the progression of events necessary to reach the point of the "Final Farewell".

The equation of which I write is easy to understand and is as follows

Acceptance minus Final Farewell equals Eternity

(acceptance − final farewell = eternity)

I MUST BEGIN WITH THE FACT THAT I AM NOT A MATHEMATICIAN. THE EQUATION mentioned is only for reference to what is needed to have eternal life with MY LORD JESUS. I will, in my feeble way, attempt to explain each part of the equation, including, the mathematical symbols and what is required for each.

As is easily seen, it is NOT an algebraic or a numerical equation. It is words that if accepted and adhered could equal a life of immense peace and tranquility, eternal life.

It will be easy for someone to NOT believe the words I write henceforth. That is understandable. Just keep in mind, IF I am wrong, I have lost nothing but some bad habits, which could have led me to an early grave BUT if I am right consider very close WHAT YOU MAY LOSE. The choice, as given to you by GOD, is and always will be yours and yours alone.

In this life, it is easy to sit back and not do anything. The government encourages exactly that, by providing very little incentive to work and rely solely upon the government for ALL needs. To be perfectly clear, I am NOT against the government "helping" those in NEED of assistance, I emphasis NEED, or assisting those after working many years, are at the age to retire, ASSISTANCE in their retirement; these individuals have over many years, according to laws passed by the government, contributed to that retirement which is not adequate for any kind of lifestyle.

The KEY is AFTER working, NOT instead of working. Exceptions would be the individual that due to a circumstance beyond the control of THAT individual such as an accident on the job, a precondition prior to the working age or a PERMANENT disability all of which would prevent the individual from working at a sustainable occupation, these need assistance.

Any person physically and or mentally capable of employment, a living income should NOT be provided. Then if employed, through no fault of their own, there is a loss of employment, assistance should be provided however for a very limited time and amount, an amount NOT sufficient to pay all the bills but only sustain life.

As long as the government provides for the income of the individual, that individual is subject to the whims and restrictions of that government and there is NO real or permanent security.

Security for a fact, in this life, on this earth, is anything but secure. There is no longer anyplace that safe from those for one reason or another want to take what individual has or even take the person's life. The areas once believed to be SAFE—our homes, our children in school and even our bank accounts have become vulnerable to a portion of the population of whom want nothing more than to TAKE instead of work it out for themselves. The sad result is that we who have worked most of our lives to be able to enjoy life must now watch everywhere we may go, even in our homes, and take precautions to protect anything and everything we have acquired through our lives, even our children!

Life IN Jesus is secure, even if there is someone willing to kill, the most is no more than a transfer from this world to a much better and secure world. That is NOT to say a person should run out and try to get killed, "YOU SHALL NOT PUT THE LORD YOUR GOD TO THE TEST." It does say, the most they can do is kill and we MUST continue to live in this world UNTIL called by *JESUS* to "Come Home!"

What those who would do harm to another person should FEAR is "It is an awesome thing to be in the hands of a LIVING GOD," and, "Vengeance is mine say the LORD." The words are paraphrased but is what the Bible states very plainly.

ACCEPTANCE

The first part of the equation is acceptance. Acceptance means willingly receive; willingly receive the sacrifice that Jesus made for the forgiveness of sins, because, GOD, the father, gave and then willing received the sacrifice HIS only SON as atonement for any and all sins. The sins of everyone were paid in full; the only thing left to do is ACCEPT it, to willingly receive.

Jesus died the cruelest death man has ever devised. He was first beaten until HIS back was a bloody mess then, to be stretched and hung on a wooden cross, arms outstretched, nails pounded through the hands and feet and then left to hang with blood draining from the body, extremely difficult to breathe; it amounted to a very slow and painful death, a most torturous death to be sure. This DEATH, JESUS willingly endured to be an acceptable sacrifice, so that your sins and mine could be placed on HIM AND be accepted by GOD, the Father, as adequate payment, thus be removed and cast away as far as the east is from the west and NEVER considered or even thought of again.

To willingly receive into your heart is not just say "I accept". Just to say this without receiving Jesus into the heart amounts to what I call "lip service". Unfortunately many only give "lip service" and only say "I accept" because, "it's the thing to do", "because my friend says I should" or "it is a way to GET AHEAD". As a teenager I did exactly as mentioned, "because my friend…"

That is not to say I attempted to "show" others I was sincere but the new, soon wore off and I was the same as before.

"For ALL have sinned and fall short of the glory of GOD" (ROMANS 3:23 NAS) and "For GOD so loved the world, that HE gave HIS only begotten SON, that whoever believes in HIM shall not perish, but have everlasting life" (JOHN 3:16 NAS). These two scriptures have been seen and heard in one form or another for the last two thousand years. To many, they are said so often, they have become boring or worse, they close their ears to them and no longer even pay attention or when the words mentioned around them, may say "What is the big deal?", or several other comments. BUT think about them. ALL, that means EVERYONE without exception, sin and are never GOOD enough to be able to receive the Grace and LOVE; HE so wants to give and GOD still loved ALL people enough to sacrifice HIS only SON as payment for those sins. What greater LOVE could possibly be given.

I have read and heard about, in the heat of a battle, one man throwing himself on a grenade to save the lives of his friends. "Greater LOVE has no one than this, that one lay down his life for his friends" (JOHN 15:13 NAS). Jesus spoke those words prior to dying on the cross, a most painful death, two thousand years ago.

The difference between "lip service" and a true commitment: there is a change in the life of the individual, what I sometimes refer to as a change in my "want to". The things I used to do I no longer "want to." A choice must be made, GOD has given everyone the "right of choice".

When the GRACE of GOD is accepted by the individual, with the heart, there is a change, the things that were a pleasure no longer are pleasurable or neither are they of any interest. A person does not want to do the things he or she did before, "The Wants Change". How does a person acquire this change? It is simple, but in order for the person to have the choice, many years and much HAD to happen.

To begin, there must be a beginning. GOD is omniscient, "has knowledge of everything". GOD knew BEFORE creation, the man HE would create would fail. God created the universe and this world with full knowledge of when man was created, "in HIS image" and gave him (man) domination of the world, because HE gave the man the right to chose, man would "listen" to outside suggestions and make wrong choices. The question is why did GOD create man if HE knew? The answer is GOD wanted fellowship with man but wanted man to *WANT* to have fellowship with HIM. To do this man had to be given the right to choose and make decisions. Forced LOVE is not love, either between GOD and man or between people.

From the very beginning, when Adam violated the one rule given him AND, I believe, failed to repent of the wrongdoing but only blamed someone else for his error, SIN entered the world. The creation was no longer as GOD had spoken, "VERY GOOD" but had to be made right again. It took four thousand years AND the sacrificial death of HIS only SON to provide a way of atonement. "And according to the LAW, *one may* almost *say*, all things are cleansed with blood, and without shedding of blood there is no forgiveness" (HEBREWS 9:22 NAS). The italics were added by the translators and the "almost" was because a few items could be cleaned with water such as eating utensils and clothing.

MINUS

The minus is the elimination for the words the believer will **NEVER** hear. To accept Jesus as the sacrifice for sins and thus will not (minus) place the individual in the position to hear the "final farewell". In place of those words, the believer will hear "Welcome true and faithful servant, enter into the joy of the kingdom." In order to explain the "final" words, I must tell who, where and how this was and WILL be accomplished. The following was a separate manuscript, however, through the "prompting" of the HOLY SPIRIT, the other (manuscript) was added to this one to give more clarity overall.

FINAL FAREWELL

BEFORE I BEGIN, IT IS MY DESIRE TO INDICATE JUST HOW THIS ALL BEGAN. What follows was the most further thing on my mind as I prepared and went to bed THAT one Sunday evening.

It was two thirty A.M. (2:30 A.M.) Monday morning. I was awakened with a word in my mind, "Good-Bye". At the very first I was puzzled but quickly became excited and extremely happy! My thoughts were, "I am saying good-bye to this world, the pain, agony and turmoil that it produces in abundance. My Lord was telling me to say good-bye to all the heartaches and chaos and COME HOME!" I was more than ready BUT nothing happened. Then for a second time there were the words, "Final Goodbye"!

I considered these words, disappointed I was NOT leaving this world after all to be with my loved ones and my LORD JESUS CHRIST.

I heard my grandfather clock chime four times; it was four A.M. (4 A.M.) before I was able to go back to sleep.

When I awoke it was daylight. I wondered what it could possibly mean, "Goodbye" or for that matter "Final Goodbye". I thought about it as I did my necessary daily chores but nothing seemed to make any sense.

I was watching one of the VERY few television programs that I DO watch. It was a Bible teacher who explains the scriptures, verse by verse. As he was explaining a section of the Bible, he referenced the verse in the book of MAT-

THEW: "Then he said to those on his left, Depart from Me, accursed ones, into the eternal fire which has been prepared for the devil and his angels" (MATTHEW 25:41 NAS). The portion of the scripture which seemed to jump out of the television was "depart from me, accursed ones."

THAT WAS IT! The fog suddenly cleared; it was perfectly clear! I KNEW what I was supposed to do! I hurried to my computer and began to type the following:

I MUST state a disclaimer. As I refer to the various individuals in the Bible, I must admit I "WILL" be using my imagination as to what may have been said or what might have been done. Of course, I have no way of knowing the mind of the individual or for that matter what they may have actually were thinking at the time. The only fact stated in the Bible is the actual leaving of the individual. It must be remembered, each one is as "I" imagined and it may NOT have been exactly the way it actually happened. The method or type of "goodbye" may actually be different because of the customs or traditions of the time and also may be affected by the gender of the person. I must rely upon my experience, the observation of others and as mentioned my imagination.

I'll begin with the simple goodbye. It is something we learn about the time we begin to form words like Ma Ma or Da Da. As a young child, not even able to walk yet, the child being held in the arms of a parent, the parent then waves a little arm at a departing person and says to the child, "Say bye-bye!"

From that time and for the rest of the person's life; life is filled with saying "good-bye" in one form or another. There are happy and sad ones, those that are carefree and those that are grievous. There are even those that are "glad they are gone and hope they never come back" types.

Every language has some word for good-bye. It can be "so long", "see ya" or "get lost!" in this country. In Spain, they may say, "Adios", in France, "Au Revoir", in Japan, "Sayonara", if in Germany you may say, "auf Wiedersehen", in Russia, "Do Suidaniya", but the Zulus in Africa say, "Hamba Kahle" or in England you may hear "Cherrio". Every country has a way to say goodbye and many times it is the inflection of the voice or the accent on a certain syllable that makes the determination and may even change the meaning. For instance, in Israel a Hebrew may say Shalom which translated means "peace". Shalom is both a greeting of hello AND a way to say goodbye depending on the inflection of the voice. In case you are wondering, I am NOT a person that knows or can even speak any of these languages. In my travels over this world, I have had the privilege to speak to many people from different parts of the world, but I learned very little of the languages. The above is about the extent of my skill, except perhaps, maybe a few other words.

The following are, in my opinion, as I read the Bible, different TYPES and ways the various individuals of the Bible MAY have said "goodbye".

As I began a study of the scriptures, I was amazed to find the number of times the people of the Bible HAD to leave, without actually saying those exact words but with only an indication of the reason for leaving. One way of saying goodbye without verbally a word being spoken is to simply turn your back to the other person and walk away. According to what I read in the Bible, this is how GOD said it, in many cases, grieved or with sadness, and of course without walking away but just turning HIS back. From all the indications I have read in the Bible, you DID NOT want GOD to turn HIS back on you!

Those involved *KNEW* when GOD turned HIS back on them; their lives changed for the worse, foreign nations invaded the land, citizens were exiles or placed into slavery, there were droughts, famines and many other things as the protection of GOD was withdrawn and they were left on their own.

The following is a very short history of the relationship of man and GOD; when it is broken by SIN and GOD *MUST* turn HIS back to say "goodbye".

For instance, consider the PAIN and SADNESS it must have caused GOD when HE knew to Adam and Eve would HAVE to leave the GARDEN, HE had prepared the GARDEN just for them and now had to force them into a world of hardship and pain because they violated the one and only rule HE had given them.GOD *IS* able to feel pain and sadness. It was NOT a pleasant way to tell the ones "made in the image of GOD", they were no longer welcome in the Garden. The actual feelings are not indicated, but I am sure GOD *MUST* have had them. Perhaps, not a physical pain as we suffer, but definitely pain, a spiritual pain; to watch his children bring unnecessary anguish upon themselves, the sadness, as HIS children made decisions which are NOT in their best interest. GOD made man "In HIS image" therefore GOD, I believe, has all the emotions the same as people. I glean from the pages of the Bible, this same concern and pain from GOD as HE looks upon the actions of HIS children today.

I had no children of "my own" but raised two from a very early age. It PAINED me greatly to see them make decisions which were NOT in their best interest but I HAD to allow them the freedom to do exactly that. It is unfortunate, we at times MUST learn from our mistakes. I had learned, but when I attempted to pass what I had learned to "my children", they found, often times too late, they should have listened and taken my advice. I am NOT saying they rebelled; it was they THOUGHT they knew a better or easier way. DAD was old fashioned and was not keeping up with the times.

I think about Adam, as he was leaving a perfect world of peace and tranquility into a world of turmoil and difficulty. The remorse and despair he must have had for violating that *ONE* rule and now HAD to say "goodbye" to it all. How sad he must have been! Adam had been told of the consequence of violating the ONE rule, which he ignored. Did he and Eve have tears in their eyes as they looked upon the beautiful GARDEN for the last time? They had only hardship, pain and turmoil in which to look forward.

I can only think of the pain I HAD when "forced" to leave the only *REAL* home I ever knew at that time of my life and my very first dog to return to a life in the "big city". I was only twelve, but I had to leave the fresh and clean air of the country to the filth and polluted air of the big city, leave my first girlfriend, a sweet, blond-haired girl and my loyal dog. My dog, who had waited at the bus stop for me every school day and never left my side when I was outside the house. My father would NOT allow me to take my dog with me to the city. I HAD to leave it all. My sadness was only compounded when I found out "my dog" had run away from the new owner. I am sure if they had looked at the bus stop where I got on and off the school bus, they would have found him, waiting for me.

Cain was forced to leave his family because of jealousy and the killing of his bother Abel. The jealousy involved a sacrifice to GOD which must have been tainted in some way and thus was rejected. The sacrifice of Abel WAS accepted. Jealousy turned into rage and Cain killed his brother, Abel, and THEN attempted to hide it from the eyes of GOD.

From the very beginning, GOD had instituted the blood sacrifice for the remission of sin. This is in evidence by the "killing" of an animal to clothe Adam and Eve when they had violated the one and only rule imposed on them. Further evidence was when Cain and Able came to sacrifice to

GOD. The sacrifice of Abel was an animal, thus was accepted, the sacrifice of Cain was not an animal, perhaps NOT even the first fruits of the crop, therefore was not accepted.

With much anxiety and nervousness about leaving, GOD had to mark him in some way to keep OTHERS from harming him. Cain said "goodbye" to his parents and other members of his family; he and his wife left for the unknown. Others? Apparently there were more offspring of Adam and Eve than Cain and Abel because Cain took with him a wife. She HAD to be the daughter of Adam and Eve.

We next come to Noah, for a hundred years, he struggled to build an Ark to save his family and the animals, plus to try and convince others of the impending disaster of a flood.

No one listened and I am sure he was ridiculed and laughed at, right up to the moment the flood began and the rain began to fall. The grief and agony he must have felt because many of his relatives, perhaps even his parents would soon perish. How many of his own brothers and sisters were among those that perished? Once GOD closed the door to the Ark, Noah knew it was all over and he would never see them again. What a sad farewell it must have been for Noah. I am left to wonder; did his wife and children, three sons and their wives actually believe destruction was going to happen, or were they obeying Noah because he was the head of the household? Regardless, destruction came and only the eight of them survived.

Next for Noah and his wife, after the flood had subsided, his three sons and their wives were to leave the Ark and venture into the world. Although nothing is said in the Bible, I am sure the parting of the family must have been difficult, at best, even if there had been problems within the family. They must had become very close during the time of the flood and were now splitting apart into a vast unknown world, and as far as they knew, they were the only people left on the earth and were told to repopulate and subdue the earth.

I remember the day I left my parents' home, the tears my mother had in her eyes as the youngest of her three sons left for an uncertain future. I think that was the first time I saw my mother cry. In her heart, she knew, although I would return for brief periods to visit, she would no longer be able see her son as often as she would like. I had told her in no uncertain terms, I would NEVER return to live in the city again, to visit, yes, but not to live. I did exactly what I said I would do! For me, it was a happy departure, I was on my own and away from the city, I had learned to despise. I did not like to see the tears of my mother but otherwise I was GLAD to "get away". I did not SAY nor would I allow my mother SAY "GOODBYE". Her tears were sufficient, and to me, at the time, goodbye would have sounded so final.

When Enoch departed, there was no fanfare, party or even a goodbye.

> "And Enoch walked with GOD; and he was not; for GOD
> took him" (GENESIS 5:21 KJV).

There may have been those that were glad to see him gone, but there is no mention of ANYONE even noticing he was gone and not around.

Abram was called by GOD to leave his family and travel to an unknown country and an uncertain future. He left his family, as instructed by God to travel to this unknown country. It would be a journey through an unknown land and people, with all the hazards, robbers and thieves to another unknown land also filled with people he knew little if anything about. Perhaps his friends and relatives gave him a "going away party". I know the "going away parties" I have attended were joyous occasions, lots of talk, laughter and wine, LOTS OF WINE, but there always came the time to say goodbye. I must also admit, there was a time or two I was GLAD to be leaving both the party and the area! Although these times were supposed to be sad, with sad goodbyes, in my heart I was glad to leave! We had a saying in the military: "The two best places in the world to be were the place you going and the last one you left." As it implies, the worst was the place you were at the time but only until you were at the next place.

After the death of his father, Abram as told by GOD to leave the country of his birth. Abram buried his father and after the proper mourning, left with his family plus his servants and merchandise he had accumulated, he was on his way to a new land. His wife Sarai and his nephew, Lot, were the only relatives mentioned.

He left the country and people he knew and a way of life for the unknown. The only things he knew was GOD had told him to go and he would make a great nation from him. I wonder, if, as he or anyone of the group, while swaying back and forth on the back of the camel, turned and reluctantly looked back and thought about whether they would EVER see any of their family or friends again. For all in the caravan, it may have been a reluctant goodbye to everything and everybody they knew.

Abram arrived in the new land, with his wife, Sarai, and his nephew, Lot. Sarai was barren and was not able to have children, and Lot, if he had a wife with him, she would not be mentioned until much later. The others mentioned were not part of the immediate family were servants and slaves.

There came a great famine in the country. Abram traveled to Egypt to escape it. Abram lied, telling the Pharaoh Sarai was his sister, which caused the Pharaoh to take her into his house. The intention, I am sure, was to make Sarai his wife or perhaps his concubine. God put a plague on Pharaoh which somehow told him that Sarai was actually the wife of Abram.

The Pharaoh was very angry and told Abram to "GET OUT" of Egypt and take Sarai and everything with him! I can only imagine the ruler of Egypt, possibly, red faced because of his blood pressure so high, a person with the power and authority to have anyone put to death without cause, literally screaming at a sheepherder to get out and stay out of Egypt. "GOODBYE! AND GET OUT OF EGYPT AND DON'T COME BACK!" The Pharaoh must have had the urge to kill BUT perhaps also knew what GOD would do IF he did.

There was one time in my life, BEFORE I was a "child of the living GOD," I became very angry. I was an enlisted airman stationed on an Air Force base in the United States. During my time in the air force, I had been cussed and discussed, ridiculed and made fun of and might even say at times verbally abused. I took it with "a grain of salt" as my thought was, if they are talking about me they are leaving someone else alone. However, there IS a line that IF ANYONE was to cross it would immediately raise my temper. That line was, IF ANYONE did ANYTHING to hurt or cause distress to someone I loved, I would react and react quickly.

This particular time, my wife was having an asthma attack so I took her to the hospital for treatment. She was called to see a doctor. I had to wait in the waiting room; spouses were not allowed, Air Force policy, to accompany them to the examination room. After waiting what I considered an extended length of time, I went looking for her.

Medics attempted to stop me, but I simply said, "I AM going to see about my wife" and pushed them aside. I found her sitting in a chair, in the hallway, crying and gasping for breath. When I ask what was wrong, she, between gasps and in almost a whisper, said the doctor had told her to sit in the hallway until SHE could tell him what was wrong. Even I could SEE the problem! I told her to hang on, I WOULD return in a few minutes and turned to walk away.

Again, medics attempted to stop me, asking where I was going. Again, I pushed them aside and told them it was none of their (expletive deleted) business. I went straight to the office of the Hospital Commander. As I entered the outer office, I was making my presence known by nearly shouting, "I want to see the hospital commander, NOW!" I only made myself more obvious to anyone when the secretary attempted to quiet me, by raising my voice even louder.

The commander came out of his office to see what all the noise was about and said to me in a rather soft but firm voice, "What seems to be the problem, son?"

I began, "SIR! I am a G.I., I signed up to be a G.I. and if you see fit to treat me with A.P.Cs. and G.I. gin, I accept. But my wife is NOT G.I. I don't expect her to be treated like royalty, but neither do I want her treated like dirt."

He asked again, "What IS the problem?" I then proceeded to tell him of the events leading to my coming to see him. His reply again in a soft but firm voice, "Well, let's go see exactly what the problem is." I honestly did not believe that he believed a doctor would do such a thing and perhaps I was not aware of the problem.

As we entered the outer waiting room, there was suddenly shouts and medics running here and there as each one instantly recognized the commander and those that did not know he was the Hospital Commander, saw the star on his shoulder and knew he was a general! Several medics attempted to intercept him and ask if there was anything they could do. His only comment was, "Follow me." He walked straight to where my wife was STILL sitting, leaned over her and spoke very softly to her. I did not venture to listen, but he suddenly turned and barked out orders to the several medics who had followed us. "YOU! Get a wheelchair! YOU! Call Major …. and tell him I WANT HIM personally to care for this lady immediately and anytime after she needs help. YOU! Take this lady to see Major… And I want her there ten minutes ago, DO YOU UNDERSTAND!" There were a chorus of YES SIRS! He then turned to me and said, "You go with her."

"Yes Sir!" As we left, I glanced back to see what was going to happen, the commander opened the door to the doctor's office, without knocking or being announced, entered. I have no idea what may have happened after that, I can only believe the doctor was immediately transferred to another location where his lack of skill would be appreciated. It was, for me anyway, a sweet, get out of here goodbye.

Moses may have had to say a very quick goodbye, if he said anything, when he thought the Pharaoh would kill him for killing an Egyptian taskmaster of the Hebrews. He fled into the desert and did not return to Egypt for forty years. Upon return to Egypt, Moses attempted to obtain a simple "so long, see you later," from Pharaoh for the Hebrews to worship GOD away from the Egyptians. Pharaoh refused to allow them to be away from their work. More requests were made but as each request was denied which was followed by some kind of plague, the simple goodbye became more prolonged and complicated UNTIL finally Pharaoh told all the Hebrews "GOODBYE and GOOD RIDENCE." To reach this point, Pharaoh and all the Egyptians had to have all their first born to die in one night.

The population of Hebrews had grown to an estimated million but rebellion to GOD also grew almost in direct proportion. A permanent and visible method of instruction from GOD, HIS rules and LAWS, had to be instituted. Moses, under the direction of GOD, wrote the rules and laws to follow and the consequences for NOT following them. Contained in the writings were the EXACT procedures and requirements for sacrifices.

The requirements of when, where and by whom, an ox, bull, goat, a lamb and sometimes doves or pigeons were to be sacrificed. The blood of each had to be placed or poured out in a specific way and at certain times of the year, for the sins of that year. IN my own opinion, it seems they could live anyway they wanted the rest of the year as long as they were able to sacrifice the one time and have all the previous sins forgiven. It was unfortunate that even this was not sufficient, "the chosen people" repeatedly turned to other gods, which were not gods but only pieces of wood or stone covered with some kind of metal.

Moses had to say farewell to the Hebrews as they were about to enter the "Promised Land", forty years later. They were forced to wander in the desert for forty years because of their rebellion. It must have been a sad farewell because he, Moses, was not allowed, by the order of GOD, because of "his" disobedience, to enter with them, he could only observe the "Promised Land" from a mountain top. In his farewell to the Hebrews, he told them AGAIN the LAWS they were to follow and the consequences if not followed. Moses died on the mountain, was buried, mourned and said goodbye, by all those present, Moses had been their "leader" for over forty years.

Joshua became the leader of the Hebrews as they entered the "Promised Land" and took possession of the land under the guidance of GOD. It may have been a relief type of goodbye, as Joshua completed the work assigned him and announced,

> "As for me and my house, we will serve the LORD" (Taken from the last sentence of JOSHUA 24:15 KJV).

I say a relief because Joshua had been their leader through all the battles in the "Promised Land". He was stepping down as their leader, into retirement, and now they were to follow *ONLY* GOD and HIS rules. The Hebrews followed "The LAW" *ONLY* as long as the elders were alive. The new generation began to follow after the gods of those they had defeated.

The Age of the JUDGES begins. The Book of Judges first mentions Caleb as a judge, but little is said other than he died and was buried on his land. The next to JUDGE the Hebrews was Othniel; the land had been at rest for forty years. Othniel was the son of the brother of Caleb and married a daughter of Caleb. Although not said, Othniel appears to be one the last "elders". Upon his death, the Bible tells of the "rebellion to the LAW" and the subjection by other nations that followed.

The next, with a brief detail of his activities, was Ehud, when the land that was invaded and ruled by the Moabites. Ehud was a Benjamite and was left-handed. Everyone wore their swords on the left side to be able to withdraw it from the sheath in a hurry with their RIGHT hand. Everyone, that is, except Ehud. Ehud made himself a dagger with two sharp edges about eighteen inches long and hid it on his RIGHT side under his cloak. On the pretense of important information for the king of the Moabites, he obtained a PRIVATE audience. Alone with the king, Ehud withdrew the hidden dagger from his right hip and plunged it deep into the king's stomach. "And Ehud put forth his *LEFT*

hand and took the dagger from his *RIGHT* thigh, and thrust it into his belly"
(JUDGES 3:21 KJV). I imagine as he plunged the dagger into the stomach of
the king, Ehud softly muttered, "SO LONG and good riddance." Then left
the dead king, hurriedly but happily and began the rebellion that freed the
Hebrews of Moabite dominion and the defeat of the oppressors of his country.
I am sure Ehud was not the only one to be happy to say "good riddance", the
rest of his countrymen were happy as well.

The next incident involves a woman. All the underlying under currents are
not explained. Only a certain man, Heber, a Kenite, had separated himself from
the rest of his clan. He was a descendent of Moses and had a wife named Jael.

Deborah, a prophetess, was leading the army of Israel against the Canaanite army because of the reluctance of the man, Barak, who was called by GOD
to lead. Deborah prophesied, because of the attitude of Barak, a woman would
obtain the glory of the battle.

For Barak, this would have been most humiliating. Not only would he not
be able to claim the victory, but a "WOMAN" would be the victor of the battle. The woman was, in that day and culture, nothing more than property and
an expense. She-goats and she-donkeys were of a higher value than a woman.
Even in our modern culture, there are still peoples in the world that consider
a woman of less importance that their animals and have gone so far as destroying baby girls as soon as they are born, literally throwing them out like so
much trash.

The Canaanite army under the command of Sisera, was defeated and because, apparently, his chariot had been severely damaged, left the battle on
foot. He arrived at the tent of Heber, exhausted, was invited into the tent by
Jael to rest. It very clear to me that GOD must have placed into the mind of
Jael the following because there had been peace between Heber and the king
of the Canaanites prior to this time.

Whatever the reason, Jael must have had a plan. She had no weapon of
any kind and even if she did, he was a soldier and could have easy overcome
her. Invited to rest, she provided him with nourishment and Sisera laid down
peacefully to rest. Jael drove a tent peg through the temple of Sisera killing
him instantly. I can almost hear Jael say, "Good night, sweet dreams."

When Barak came searching for Sisera, Jael proudly announced, "The
man you are searching for is inside, dead." Thus the Hebrews, in the area,

could say a thankful goodbye to their oppressors and *A WOMAN* was acclaimed the victor of the war.

Jephthah, a son of a harlot, was called by the elders of Gilead, to lead the men of the country into a battle with the Ammonites. To assure success, he made a vow unto the LORD. The LORD gave him success and when he returned home, his only child, a daughter, came running out of the house, with dancing and timbrels (type of musical instrument) to greet him on his successful return. This grieved Jephthah; he had vowed to sacrifice the first of what came to greet him on his successful return. When he told his daughter, she said (paraphrased), "If you had made a VOW to the LORD you must keep it." Jephthah had to tell is daughter a heartbreaking farewell but had to sacrifice her life as well. As an added note: BE VERY careful what you vow or promise the LORD. A vow to the LORD can be broken ONLY by the LORD.

I made a vow to my LORD in 1978, shortly after I had become HIS CHILD. I vowed that no alcohol would knowingly pass over my lips if HE, JESUS, would remove from me its DESIRE and hold on me. Jesus did exactly what I ask HIM to do and I have KEPT that vow to the extent that I will not even eat anything cooked with or made with alcohol. Alcohol had destroyed the occupation I loved, almost destroyed my family and could have destroyed my very life as well, had I continued. My interpretation of my vow may seem overly severe on my part, it was MY choice. GOD has given everyone the right of choice, I chose to exercise THAT right to this day.

Gideon was the next judge and waged a successful war against the Midians. When asked to rule, it appears Gideon gave a humble no and goodbye, left to "retire" in peace.

Samson was the next to the last of the Judges. After several encounters with the Philistines, he was finally drained of his strength, by the intrigue and the cutting of his hair by a woman, was thus captured and blinded. For a celebration and sacrifice to their god Dagon, the Philistines brought Samson into the arena to "make sport" of him. HE was secured between two pillars, where the audience could laugh at and make fun of him, the Philistines either forgot or perhaps failed to notice his hair, the symbol and reason of his strength, had grown to some length.

As Samson pulled the roof of the arena down upon himself and all the Philistines, he said his final good bye, "Then Samson called to the LORD and said, O Lord GOD, please remember me, and please strengthen me, just this time, O GOD, that I may be at once be avenged of the Philistines for my two eyes" (JUDGES 16:28 NAS). Thus with a vengeful good bye Samson pulled down the pillars of the temple of Dagon, died and killed about three thousand men and women at the same time.

Samuel was the last judge of Israel and after him was the reign of the kings. In the case of Samuel, it was not Samuel that said goodbye to the people, but the people to say goodbye to Samuel. The people no longer wanted him to "judge" them but wanted a king to rule over them. GOD informed Samuel it was not him, they were rejecting (goodbye), but GOD, HIMSELF. The people no longer wanted GOD to rule but someone else, a human person.

Samuel, under the direction of GOD, explained the problems which would occur by naming a king. The response was, "We want to be like the other nations around us." Samuel, therefore, again with the direction of GOD selected and anointed a man named Saul. When made king, Samuel bid a sad goodbye and left for retirement. His broken heart and sadness in the goodbye was not for him leaving them as much as they were leaving the rule and direction of GOD, as a Prophet of GOD I am sure GOD had given him the insight of what was to happen. They were rejecting the one true and everlasting king. Samuel was "called" back several more times for one reason or another, once even after he had died, by King Saul through a witch from Endor. Consulting with witches was in direct violation of the LAW given by GOD.

The disobedience of Saul precipitated the next goodbye. Saul had been instructed by GOD to destroy all the Amalekites, every person, all the livestock and much of the material items. His disobedience involved keeping the "best of the livestock" for sacrifice, the soldiers were allowed to take booty and even allowing the king of the Amalekites, to remain alive. To compound his disobedience, Saul decided he would take the place of Samuel and perform the sacrifice. This was ONLY to be done by a priest, in this case should have been Samuel, he was a priest as well as a prophet.

Samuel arrived to witness the proceedings and with anger and pain at this direct disregard for the WORD of GOD, AGAIN said goodbye to Saul, but not before he killed the king of the Amalekites and chopped the body into several parts. This time Saul never again looked upon the face of Samuel, until Samuel was conjured up by the witch of Endor, it was a last goodbye.

Samuel was told by GOD to anoint David to be king. Because of the exploits of David and it was recognized by Saul that GOD was no longer with him and was now with David; Saul began a campaign to destroy David. David had to flee for his life. The following are the various ways and individuals David had to say goodbye.

Saul attempted to say "goodbye" by sending David on dangerous missions in hopes of the Philistines would kill David, but instead, David was successful which only made David more popular with the people; Saul then tried to kill him with a spear as they sat to eat. David HAD to leave in a hurry, no doubt a very quick "maybe I'll see you later".

While David was with his wife, Michal, Saul sent men to bring David to him so he could kill him. Michal let David escape by way of a window and then faked a medical problem to delay his escape. It must have been a quick "I love you" and shalom (peace).

During the following years of hide and evade with Saul, David had to flee for his life and say to Jonathon, the son of Saul, a heartbreaking good bye, to Ahimeleah, a priest, a reluctant and a cautious farewell because he knew there was a spy close by, to Achish, the king of Gath, in fear, when David faked being a madman, to the king of Moab and his own family with sadness as he left them in protective custody and a thankful good bye to Abigail for preventing him from destroying another human unnecessarily.

Saul finally gave up the chase when David proved his loyalty to him by NOT killing Saul when he had the chance. Saul issued a final farewell to David.

Afterward Saul was killed in battle, David became king of Israel. Even as king, David was not immune to sad goodbyes. The son born to him by Bathsheba, because the son was conceived while Bathsheba was married to another, the baby became very sick. David fasted and prayed for the life of the child for seven days. When the child died, David rose and assumed normal life, when ask why. He said, "But now he is dead, wherefore should I fast? Can I bring him back to life again? I shall go to him but he shall not return to me" (II SAMUEL 12:23 KJV). A note: This is the first mention, in the Bible, of a resurrection and a joining with our loved ones.

Absalom, his son attempted to assume the position of king while David was still alive but was killed in the attempt. David was in a state of mournful goodbye as he walked around shouting,

"O my son Absalom, my son, my son Absalom! Would I had died instead of you. O Absalom, my son, my son!" (2 SAMUEL 18:33 NAS).

David ruled for forty years, as he became old and it was time to have his son, Solomon, to be king, the goodbye was both elaborate and detailed. It was a matter of a fact type of goodbye. It was, "I leave you to do this and see that this is done and use your own wisdom to accomplish this, don't forget about this." It was expected, Solomon, as his son, to follow the instructions of the father even if the son was now the king. Solomon followed the directions of his father, David, to the letter.

Rehoboam became king after his father Solomon died. One of the first acts, as king, caused the split of the twelve tribes of the Hebrews into ten tribes of Israel and two tribes of Judah. The ten tribes said, "What portion do have we with David? We have no inheritance in the son of Jesse; To your tents, O Israel" (I KINGS 12:16b NAS). In the present-day language, "So long, its be good to know you, don't call us we'll call you."

All but three of the kings of Judah were mourned (goodbye) and buried with "their fathers". Of the three, one was taken as captive to Egypt and the other two taken to Babylon. Two that were taken to Babylon; one appears to have died in prison and the last one was released and became a guest at the king's table. Nothing is said of anyone mourning their deaths and all three apparently were buried in a foreign land.

During the reign of the kings of Israel and Judah, there were many prophets, those who recorded, in writing, their prophesies and those only mentioned by name or deeds. With very few exceptions, most were met with an untimely death at the hands of the very ones they were trying warn of the disaster to come, if changes were not made. They were ridiculed and maligned by the kings and elders. Few if any were mourned, at least openly, and most of the people cheered and were happy to be rid of what they determined to be a pest. It is a sad turn of events, when a person leaves, either in death or just to walk out the door with NO ONE to mourn or say a kind goodbye.

After my second wife had died, I was examining the many things she left behind. I found, tucked away in a small corner of a drawer, a diary. Curious, I began to read the various entries. Most were about this or that until I came upon an entry which broke my heart. Years before she even knew I existed, it was a very unhappy time in her life. It seems all her children had rejected her and wanted NOTHING to do with her. Her entry stated, "I fear that when I die there will be NO ONE to be by my bed side or even mourn my passing."

I knew NOTHING of this diary or its entry when, after being notified my beloved had only twenty-four hours to live, I telephoned all her children and grandchildren to come to her side. I had each one, while she still able to hear, to talk to her PRIVATELY. When she breathed her last breath on this earth, she had not only myself but all her children and grandchildren by her side. Without realizing what I had done, I had relieved her of THAT fear. I will admit, I did it for selfish reasons. I did it because I did NOT want anyone screaming or wailing at the funeral about not having an opportunity to tell her of their feelings or the opportunity to say "goodbye". I had heard such, so many times from the very people, who when the deceased was living, would not so much as give the deceased the time of day and I did NOT want anyone to have any excuse to say, "I didn't have a chance to…".

JOB did not have a chance to say farewell to his children. Job was a very wealthy man with large herds of cattle and sheep; he was respected and upright. Satan came and destroyed all he had including his ten children. It all came about so quickly. Job did not realize what was happening until it was all over. How he must have mourned, when it became obvious to what extent was his loss and without even a chance to say anything to or for his children.

I know how painful it is to HAVE to say goodbye to a loved one. I sat next to my mother and my sweet mother-in-law when they died, watched my father take his last breath and I sat and held the hands of both my wives, watched as the life of each ebbed away, they take their last breath and NOT BE ABLE to do even the smallest thing to stop it or help them in any way. It is impossible for me to write how my heart was breaking, the pain I felt. I can only say, as each died, a part of me died. My wives and I had become ONE while they lived. When they died, a huge part of me was torn from my being; the pain was beyond description. However, there was also a sense of relief, because they no longer had to endure the pain of the sickness they had for the last *YEARS* of their life on this earth. It took literally years for me to recover enough to continue or even want to and I still, after all these years, have times of difficulties which are hard to explain.

During the times of the kings, the Israelis rebelled time after time. While in rebellion, GOD sent numerous prophets to announce the error of their ways, and if change was not forthcoming there would be disaster to follow. For the most part, the warnings were ignored, the prophets beaten, killed and thrown into prison. In the case of Jeremiah the Prophet, he was thrown into a well.

There is one prophet, I will mention, Elijah, mostly because of the circumstances involved. According to the seventeenth chapter of I KINGS, it begins with Elijah pronouncing a severe drought upon the nation because of the sins of the nation that would last three and half years. Elijah leaves King Ahab and runs into the wilderness to hide from the wrath, NOT of the king, but his wife, Jezebel. After, under the direction of GOD, being fed there by ravens and the brook from which he was drinking dried up because of the drought, he was then directed to a town called Zarephath. It is here that a strange occurrence takes place. He is directed to meet with a widow. The widow is picking up sticks to prepare the last meal for her son and herself. It was going to be her last goodbye to her son as she cooked their last meal.

Before I continue, I believe there is a need to explain the situation as I see it. The widow is apparently young or at least the child is very young. I say this because the male child was the inheritor of the property WHEN he became of age, it was, in that culture, the age of twelve. It appears the son had not reached the age yet OR perhaps, the debts mentioned were so great that there was no inheritance left for him.

In either case, she was preparing to eat the last meal and die. Elijah, appearing heartless, tells her to make for him something to eat instead HER last meal. Instead of the little flour being exhausted with the last little bit cooked, the bowl of flour remained full and the oil never failed until the drought had subsided. She even filled enough extra bowls and containers for her to pay all her creditors as well.

What has this to do with the goodbyes? The widow had already said the goodbye for herself and to her son, as she was prepared to cook and eat the last meal and die. What a sad event for her and her son it must have been, the end of the family line and no one apparently cared. Another incident will be stated, similar in nature but involving JESUS and will be mentioned later.

In the chapters of the Bible following this, the last of chapter twenty and chapter twenty-one, it tells about King Ahab, king of Israel. As a king, he had the power to put to death anyone who opposed him. King Ahab confronts two, an unnamed prophet and a man named Naboth. Both opposed him but instead of being the king that he was, King Ahab turned, a form of goodbye, and left them "vexed and sullen". In the modern way of speaking, he left like "a dog with its tail tucked between its legs". It seems to me, this "king" was still, mentally, a child. It took his "dominant" wife, Jezebel, to solve the problem, at least with Naboth.

The prophets came and many died very untimely death at the hands of the kings and elders they were trying to help. Except for a few, the Bible does not say how each had died, only one was mourned by another prophet.

Those that were mentioned, Elijah was taken to heaven in a chariot of fire, one was killed by a bear, one was killed between the altar and the Temple by a sword or were stoned to death and not mentioned in the Bible, but tradition has it that Isaiah was SAWN in two by King Manasseh. WHY were they mistreated? They were trying to tell the people to repent, return to GOD before disaster came upon them. To be a "child of GOD" is NOT an easy life.

Disaster came; the Temple and the city were completely destroyed. The population, most of what was left, after nearly a year long siege, were exiled and taken captive to a foreign land. Only the poorest of those remaining were left to tend the flocks and the vineyards.

How absolutely sad it must have been for those being taken away "in chains" to say goodbye with much moaning and tears, to see the destruction of their beloved Temple and city. For most, they would NEVER see their homeland again and would be buried in a foreign land, which for the JEW, at the time, was almost a fate worse than death.

The Book of Lamentations, written by Jeremiah the Prophet, tells of the heartbreak, tears and pain as he experienced the destruction of his beloved city and the Temple of GOD. All the explaining to those in the city of the disaster which was coming fell on deaf ears. It must have been doubly painful for him to say "goodbye" and watch the city and Temple burn.

After seventy years of EXILE, with the decree from a more benevolent king, a small remnant returned to the "Promised Land". It must have been a very happy goodbye with the departure from a land of slavery and exile to return to the land of their forefathers.

What has been written is only a brief history of the Old Testament as it relates to what I "think" the people may have and the way they said "GOOD-

BYE". All died in one way or fashion, some had time to say the final words, some did NOT. They did, as we must, face the reality of dying. Life is nothing more than a wisp of smoke, you see it and suddenly it is no more. It does not matter if it is a baby brought into this world and only a few days old or someone who has been around and is over a hundred years old, death comes to EVERYONE. It can be sudden without warning or prolonged over a period of time; it is inevitable to every breathing soul. The question becomes, what happens after the body dies?

The prophets told of the coming Messiah, which the remnant of Hebrews who were left after the complete destruction of Jerusalem and the Temple, took to heart and began LOOKING for the Messiah. They looked for four hundred years and the Messiah did appear exactly as predicted, on time and at the very place the prophets had said.

John the Baptist preceded the Messiah, EXACTLY as predicted by the prophets. He preached the coming of the Messiah as "one crying in the wilderness" to make way for the coming "Lamb of GOD". He even pointed directly at Jesus as the Messiah, as the one who takes away the sins of the world. John the Baptist was put in prison because of his opposition to the actions of the king.

He said his goodbye, when, "Summoning two of his disciples, John sent them to the LORD, saying, "Are you the Expected One, are do we look for someone else?" (LUKE 7:19 NAS). I believe, John the Baptist KNEW Jesus was the one they had been looking for and the request would be his way of saying "goodbye" to HIM, JESUS, for as a prophet knew his time on earth was coming to a close.

Despite exact predictions and the fulfilling of those predictions, the ruling class of religious leaders of the time refused to believe Jesus WAS the Messiah. HE walked the country healing the sick, raising the dead and preaching the coming "Kingdom of GOD". The ruling class, who should have recognized HIM from the scriptures as the Messiah, only criticized, ridiculed and finally had HIM killed. All of which was also prophesied.

Why was it that the ruling religious leaders were not able or did not want to recognize their Messiah? The reason, I believe, is that although they saw the miracles preformed, their eyes were blinded in that they only saw someone attempting to remove them from their position of authority and prestige.

> "Make the heart of this people fat; and make their ears heavy,
> and shut their eyes; lest they see with their eyes and hear with
> their ears, and understand with their heart and convert and
> be healed" (ISAIAH 6:10 KJV).

How exactly could this have happened to the "chosen people"? Over the preceding years, I believe, Satan had infiltrated the hearts and minds of the religious leaders. Who instead of representing GOD in their actions, wanted the approval, esteem and respect from the people more than from GOD. This was so firmly entrenched in their thoughts and way of life; they became extremely jealous of any attempt to remove their status, even from their own Messiah. This absolutely amazing to me, however at least some of them KNEW, or at least partially believed JESUS was THE MESSIAH. Nicodemus, a ruler of the Jews (a man of a high position), came to see Jesus and said, "Rabbi, we *KNOW* that thou art a teacher *COME* from GOD; For no man can do these miracles that thou doest, except GOD be with him" (JOHN 3:2b KJV) (The italics are mine).

Was Nicodemus speaking of all the JEWS or was he speaking only of himself and maybe a few others? It appears Satan had closed the eyes and ears of the greater portion of the "JEWS", but a few were able to avoid the works of Satan.

Jesus had performed many miracles, healing the sick, casting out demons and even feeding five thousand men and their families with a couple of fish and a few loaves of bread. The miracle of raising someone from the dead had not EVER been done. This incident was alluded to previously with Elijah. The seventh chapter of LUKE beginning with the eleventh verse tells of Jesus approaching the city of Nain. Being carried out for burial was a man, THE ONLY SON of a widow. Jesus saw her and had compassion for her, walked to the coffin, said to her, "Do not weep." He touched the coffin and the man suddenly became alive and Jesus GAVE him back to his mother. Again the widow must have already said her goodbye and was concerned about her life to follow as her source of livelihood was going to be buried and there would be no one to provide for her. She had only a life of poverty and distress of which to look forward.

As a note, Jesus was never anywhere by chance. HE *IS* always at the right place at *EXACTLY* the right time. If it seems Jesus is not listening to your prayers, be rest assured the answer will EXACTLY on time. "Wait upon the LORD."

As Jesus walked this earth, HE told of HIS death and resurrection. HE was telling HIS disciples goodbye but I WILL return. None, even after HE was executed, was buried and rose from the dead, believed HE had risen from the dead and were only convinced when they saw HIM suddenly appear in a room in which ALL the doors and windows were shut and locked.

I believe there has been a misconception among some, that the Hebrews, Jews or Israelis, whatever you may want to call them, killed their Messiah. The Romans actual killed JESUS; the Hebrews only forced the issue by threat of a riot. A riot would have invoked the wrath of Rome upon the governor of Jerusalem at the time. The fear of ROME was paramount; it would have been not only to remove him from his position and prestige as governor but also to condemn him to a life of possibly total exile and outcast among the prestigious people of the Roman Empire—if he had been allowed to live at all.

As Jesus spoke on HIS last days on this earth, He spoke of not only leaving but HE would return. We, in this day and time, would tell others "See you later." It was NOT a last farewell but only a temporary separation. JESUS will return! Jesus WILL issue the FINAL "GOODBYE" and with it total separation later.

After Jesus was resurrected, HE told HIS disciples what they were to do and gave them the POWER to accomplish the task. This was HIS "see you later" speech and He ascended into Heaven. The power was the HOLY SPIRIT, who came to indwell them and every believer since that time. Without the HOLY SPIRIT, which is the very Spirit of GOD, no one can do anything for the "Kingdom of GOD".

The Bible, the New Testament, in the Book of Acts, tells of the disciples of Jesus, what they said and what they did to further the Kingdom of GOD—*NOTE*: "the Kingdom of GOD", not the Gospel or even Christianity. Several recorded miracles that a "normal" person could never accomplish, the trials and tribulations encountered in the effort to spread the GOSPEL of the coming Messiah. First to the JEWS, GOD's chosen people, when rejected, would be spread to what the Bible refers to as Gentiles, uncircumcised, heathens or Pagans. "To the Jew first and then the Gentiles."

Many were martyred. Stephen, the first, was "stoned" to death for his words spoken to the Jews. Afterward, there were some thrown into prison, killed with a sword, and fed to wild animals. John was boiled in oil and Peter was crucified upside down. If anyone had a reason NOT to believe or even doubt what Jesus said, it was the first converts to this NEW way of life. These were tortured and gave their lives for the belief there was a life AFTER the body dies.

Another example is Saul, later renamed Paul. He was a man who was determined to exterminate the belief in the resurrected Christ. He was changed by Jesus into the complete opposite person. He became even more determined to explain to any and all who would listen about Jesus. The result was he was beaten with rods, whipped with a whip, stoned and left for dead, shipwrecked and thrown into prison and finally beheaded. Paul, in his writings, is the first to mention the Gospel and also it was during this time believers in Jesus as the Messiah were called Christians. The Gospel simply stated is the belief in the death, burial and resurrection of JESUS the SON of the Living GOD.

Paul had to say goodbye to many during his journeys in what is called missionary trips. He would establish a "church", remain to firmly establish the brotherhood and move on to the next project. Many as he left, he must have told he would return, "See you later", but there was one incident that IS recorded in the Bible of his departure.

According to ACTS 20, Paul was traveling back to Jerusalem and had stopped at a town of Miletus. He sent for and gathered there, elders from Ephesus and others. It was here he gave warnings about coming events and the people not of the faith, also mentioned was he would not be returning: "You will no more see my face."

> "And they began to weep aloud and embraced Paul and repeatedly kissed him, grieving especially over the words which he had spoken, that they would not see his face again. And they were accompanying him to the ship" (ACTS 20:37-38 NAS).

What a grievous and tearful goodbye it must have been, so many MEN kneeling on the ground, praying and crying because Paul would not return but also fully aware of the fate which awaited Paul at Jerusalem.

Years later, in a letter to Timothy, some of his final words were, "to be absent from the body is to be present with the LORD." Of the apostles, ALL were martyred save John, of whom, it is believed died a natural death while in prison on the Isle of Patmos.

All the followers of CHRIST were subject to treatment of the same nature but maybe not over the long period of time and to the extent of Paul. Every Jew who accepted the WORD was thrown out of the synagogue, disowned by their family or even killed by another family member. The Jewish leaders sought to throw as many as possible into prison and to be left there indefinitely.

When the government became involved, followers of CHRIST, because they refused to bow to any other god but the true GOD, were executed, banished from cities and towns and even fed to wild animals for sport. In my opinion, Satan was doing its very best to stop the worship of the true GOD and was using every means possible. The actual result was to increase and expand the very worship it (Satan) wanted—into the worship of "THE ONLY TRUE GOD".

Government officials could not understand and wrote in official correspondence to Rome their unbelief of these people as they were tortured and executed. "These followers of CHRISTOS" went to their death singing and rejoicing. They were astounded to hear women, with their babies in their arms, singing and praising GOD as they were buried ALIVE or listen, as another would praise the HOLY GOD as he or she was being slowly killed with a sword or with some other form of torture. It was their way of saying goodbye to this world and hello to a new life and a new world.

They even, when they found they could not kill John, one of the original disciples, by boiling him in oil, they exiled him to the island prison of Patmos. Even exiled, John could not be silenced; he wrote the last book of the NEW TESTAMENT, the book of REVELATION.

The reason for all the above is Satan and its war against GOD and any and all who CHOSE to follow GOD. GOD has no desire to see anyone perish, that means to be eternally separated from HIS love and care. By contrast, Satan wants all the worship and does not care how many perish in the process.

GOD, the Father, had given every human the right to choose. HE did this because, from the very beginning, HE, GOD, did not want anyone to be COMPELLED to love HIM but to do it willingly. GOD will NOT force anyone into a relationship with HIM! Because of SIN, GOD HAD to provide a way of choice, a way to eliminate sin from the person and still remain true to HIS own written word and promises.

As I mentioned, this is a war, a war for the hearts and m minds of people. This is a war that has been in progress for over six thousand years. This is what is referred to in the Bible as a "spiritual war". I have given a brief overview of that war up to the arrival of the Messiah. Next I will attempt to provide with the various ways good bye was said as a different phase of the war begins.

For the next three hundred years, although Christianity spread across three continents, within the Roman Empire, it was severely persecuted. It was spread quickly because of the easy roadway system provided by the Roman government, built to expedite troops to any part of the empire. The universal use of the Greek language for business and all types of communications provided an easy way to spread the WORD. These had to be and were in place before the Messiah was to appear, for the first time.

Many Christians had to say goodbye to friends and relatives with tears and sadness as they were dragged off to be part of "Roman games". The games were not only to feed wild animals, as most think about, but also became targets for soldiers for practice, to enhance the skill of the soldier and to improve the method of the attack on any adversary. When these "games" became "boring", persecution did not end; it took on a different method. The Christian became a source of illumination for others to be able to walk the roadways at night. They were burned on wooden crosses. Literally thousands died this way, each saying goodbye to this world for a far better life. The persecution lasted for hundreds of years, until King Constantine declared Christianity the official religion of the empire in 312 A.D. Satan seemed to have lost a battle, but the war was far from being over.

Suddenly there was a large influx of "new" Christians. Former pagans and idolaters, many of the most vocal in the persecution of Christians, because of possible persecution, suddenly said goodbye to their former religion and embraced a new one. Perhaps they did not feel their multiple gods were strong or good enough for which to die. For whatever reason, they brought with them many of the practices and ideas of idolatry.

Satan had changed from external destruction to destruction from within. Very simply, it was through the "new" recruits, the pure Christian way of worship was infiltrated by pagan worship especially on the "holidays". As I continue, there will be those that think I am wrong or maybe should keep my ideas to myself. First let me say there is nothing wrong about celebrating a holiday, especially one concerning my LORD. My objection is the WAY it is celebrated. My LORD has given me and everyone the right of choice; I exercise that GOD given right.

Easter, the day to be celebrated, is the resurrection of my LORD. The way it IS celebrated is with, of all things, a rabbit that lays eggs, colored eggs at that. I have been told it was for the children; if that is the case, why not celebrate a rabbit that lays eggs on some other day, why have it on the ONLY day of the year in which MY LORD WAS RESURRECTED. Even the name is pagan. Easter is derived from the goddess Eastre, goddess of fertility, hence the rabbit and the laying of eggs. The rabbit is a symbol of proliferation and the eggs are the symbol of a beginning of a life. NOT A NEW LIFE IN CHRIST JESUS, just a new life!

Another day I am told is for the children, Christmas. CHRISTMAS actually means DAY of CHRIST. It is the day to celebrate the BIRTH of Christ, the Messiah. It has been turned into a day of who can give or get the biggest, most expensive or best present. "John gave me… last year, I need to give him…"

Instead of it being on the day of worship and thanksgiving for the birth of the Messiah, why not have the celebration of giving presents two weeks earlier or sometime later? Why must all the trees, lights and decorations, that are pagan inspired, be on the day of celebration of the birth of MY MESSIAH? Is it the ONLY day of the year in which a child can receive a gift of a toy?

Then there is the idea of some "fat" character, in a red suit, flying through the air, on a sled pulled by reindeer. Again I am told it is for the children. OK, then have this character fly through the air on the fifteenth of January or any other time of the year.

I personally said GOODBYE to this form of celebration many years ago and worship my LORD in a very simple way, with a special meal and much prayer of praise and thanksgiving.

Forgive me for digressing into an area which causes me pain to watch. Not only non-believers, which if that is what they want to do, that is fine, but professing Christians, believers in the Messiah Jesus, have become overwhelmed by the mass advertisements for things, many of which, will be discarded within a few months. Many, believers and unbelievers, "go into debt" to buy THINGS of which the recipient only returns to the store for something else or places into a closet to be thrown away months or years later.

It should the happiest of time of the year. IT IS A TIME to be happy but not because of the gifts or the decorations. The happiness should be this is a day in which the SAVIOR of the world was born or at least this the day of which we celebrate. In my heart, I wish this day would be celebrated on a day most nearly aligned, IN MY OPINION, with HIS birth, in the springtime of the year.

I wish to make it perfectly clear, I am NOT judging those who wish to celebrate the holidays in this fashion. It is strictly MY OPINION and what I have observed of others over the years.

> "Therefore no one is to act as your judge in regard to food or drink or in respect to a FESTIVAL or a new moon or a Sabbath day" (COLOSSIANS 2:16 NAS). (Capitalization is only for emphasis.)

But now I must return, Christianity as a religion flourished and expanded nearly unhindered for the next seven hundred years, *EXCEPT* little by little one step at a time, the pagan style of worship was introduced. It had spread from the Middle East across the northern part of Africa and throughout Europe. The center became, of all places, ROME, the very place that had proclaimed the persecution of the early followers of Christ. The primary form was Catholicism with a man at the head called The Pope.

The Pope was designated the only one who was able to speak with and for GOD. Anything he said, any rule he thought, was "from GOD" and therefore was to be followed without question. He became so powerful, he was able to make or break kings and kingdoms by a simple decree given in the name of GOD. One decree was that only a priest or higher "KNEW" enough to interpret or even read the Bible.

To believe that only ONE person can speak to or for GOD is in DIRECT contradiction to the BIBLE. Jesus HIMSELF said, "If ye ask anything in my name, I will do it" (JOHN 14:14 KJV).

Jesus repeated the same words two more times as if to emphasis the fact that ANYONE can talk with HIM and the FATHER. It IS A FACT *ANYONE* can talk with GOD; the person does not have to have an education with all kinds of letters behind the name. You can have NO education, be a young child or a person a hundred and twenty years old. You don't even have to know any language other than the one in which you were born; GOD understands ALL languages. Latin, which is now a dead language, has been the OFFICIAL language of the Catholic hierarchy for centuries. It has only been in the last hundred years or so that the language of the country in which the person happens to be in at the time, could that language be used in the services.

My mother was a Catholic and would "take" me to the services. I remember as a young child, the Priest would say everything in Latin and I did not understand then or do I understand it today, except for a few words. I was always glad to hear the one word most familiar, AMEN!

As Catholicism spread throughout the world, more MAN-MADE rules, doctrines and ideas were added until one day a priest saw the wrong and objected. The world was changed but not without much trouble and turmoil. The power structure attempted to stamp out what was determined by them heresy. Instead of eliminating the opposition, the opposition grew and became the driving force to a new nation based on religious FREEDOM.

What has all this to do with the "Final Farewell"? Historical events MUST take place according to the scriptures; all prophesies must be fulfilled.

The religious freedom was the driving force which established the United States of America. This great nation of The United States of America HAD to take its place on the world stage, based on religious principles, so the GOSPEL of JESUS CHRIST could be spread though out all the world.

Satan began to infiltrate the simple Gospel with ideas. It was NOT enough to JUST believe in the death, burial and resurrection of the Messiah, Jesus, which IS the Gospel; there HAD to be more. This or that was also required for salvation to be assured. HOGWASH! When it appeared not to make enough impression, the next tactic was employed: DISCOUNT THE BIBLE AS THE WORD OF GOD!

It appears this has been more effective. Ministers of the Bible, preachers, teachers, the very ones who are supposed to know, tell their listeners there are errors in this or that portion of the Bible and they should be eliminated or worse, ignored. One of the biggest items is GOD could not have made the world in six days; it HAD to be millions of years. It is unfortunate, those listening to such trash believe because they have NOT investigated for themselves and have taken the words issued by those people BECAUSE they have the education and learning to know about those things. AGAIN, I SAY: HOGWASH!

History tells us of past empires and the indications of that empire on the decline. It pains me to say but those indications are increasing every day in this, the greatest nation the world has ever known. YES, I believe this nation is on the decline; however, I also believe with repentance and a change in many of our attitudes, a delay or even a reduced and, maybe, a total decline can be averted. "And if MY people who are called by MY name HUMBLE themselves and PRAY and SEEK MY FACE and turn from their wicked ways, then, I will hear from Heaven, will forgive their sin and will HEAL their land"(II CHRONICLES 7:14 NAS).

There are several indications of decline witnessed by previous "empires". One of the most "noticeable" is distraction. The government, for instance, to keep the people "happy" will provide more time and more ways "to enjoy" life.

I was a "government employee" for twenty-two years, and when I began my service we had five "holidays". There is absolutely nothing wrong with holidays, but as of today the government recognizes eleven; the only month that has no holiday is August. Distraction? Keep them happy with time off and of course extra pay.

Another distraction for government employees AND the general population as well is sports; there is nothing wrong with sports, but where national sports were only confined to three major types, football, baseball and basketball, all held at specific times of the year; there are NOW sports of some kind in every month of the year and every day of the month. This does not even take into account the HOURS spent in front of a television set or "playing video games".

These are only a few of the distractions, in an effort to keep people occupied and not "THINK" about what is going on "behind their backs". As the government and those in powerful positions gradually and methodically take away the freedoms we ONCE held so dear, what we were willing and many did, die to protect and pass on to the next generation. Unfortunately, I must also include "believers" in Christ. These are distractions from the true worship of the ONE who died to give freedom to anyone who believes. They distract, as "sports" and other distractions are talked about before and after, and I must believe, think about, during the WORSHIP service!

However, there is one prophesy that must be fulfilled. For the prophesy to come about, sadly this nation MUST say "goodbye" and turn its back on the "chosen people", Israel. At present, we as a nation support Israel; however, I hear and read about Senators and Representatives and even the President complaining about the support we furnish. ISRAEL is becoming a "thorn" in the side of many of OUR politicians. These individuals do not consider IS-RAEL IS "chosen people" of GOD.

Our reliance upon the oil supplied by some countries, which have an adverse attitude against the United States and Israel, provides them with a leverage in our attitude toward GOD's "chosen people". Our economy is heavily based on oil and the petroleum products we enjoy.

Some politicians seem to think we can say "goodbye" to all petroleum products overnight. I am sorry, it CANNOT be done. There were some people, some of those very people, at one time, discounted the value of any energy source other than oil, as environmentally unfriendly. But if those energy sources had been properly pursued, they would NOW give this nation a more reliable energy foundation. I see, in retrospect, that it must have been part of the plan of GOD.

This IS the basis of the prophesy leading up to the "FINAL FAREWELL."

Isaiah states the following, not necessarily in order of occurrence. I leave that for GOD to decide. HE KNOWS. The following, unless designated, are from the NEW AMERICAN STANDARD version of the Bible.

> "Who has believed our message? And to whom has the arm of the LORD been revealed?" (Isaiah 53:1).

> "But transgressors and sinners will be crushed together, And those who forsake the LORD shall come to an end" (Isaiah 1:28).

> "The LORD arises to contend, And stands to judge the people" (Isaiah 3:13).

From chapter five (5) verse eight (8) through verse twenty-five (25) speaks of six (6) WOES TO various unrighteous individuals.

> "Behold, the LORD lays the earth waste, devastates it, distorts its surface and scatters its inhabitants" (Isaiah 24: 1).

> "The earth will be completely laid void and completely despoiled, for the LORD has spoken" (Isaiah 24:3). *THIS IS BECAUSE*:

"The earth is also polluted by its inhabitants, for they trans-gressed laws, violated statutes, broke the everlasting covenant" (Isaiah 24:5).

"For the LORD'S indignation is against **ALL** the nations, And HIS wrath against **ALL** their armies; HE has utterly destroyed them. HE has given them over to slaughter" (Isaiah 34:2). (Emphasis are mine.)

NOTICE: ALL the nations, ALL the Armies, ALL would *HAVE* to include the United States of America!

At the end of the Millennium:

"Your dead will live. Their corpses will rise. You who lie in the dust, awake and shout for joy" (Isaiah 26:19).

"Even these I will bring to MY holy mountain and make them joyful in MY house of prayer. Their burnt offerings and their sacrifices will be acceptable on MY altar. For MY house will be called a house of prayer for all peoples" (Isaiah 56:7).

Isaiah told and wrote many other prophesies concerning coming events which I, if included, would require several more pages and only reinforce what is already said. There are more prophets of GOD that speak of coming events.

Ezekiel was a prophet of the exile. When the city of Jerusalem and the Temple were completely destroyed and the population dispersed throughout the known empire of the Babylonians, Ezekiel was exiled to Babylon.

Ezekiel spoke of and it was written in chapter thirty-eight (38) and thirty-nine (39) of his book, the coming invasion of Israel. This is a separate invasion from any so far; it involves the countries of NORTHERN Europe and Persia. Previous invasions have been from the area in and around the Middle East. Also *this* invasion will be stopped by DIVINE intervention and a tremendous loss of life will occur. The invading force WILL return to their countries WITHOUT acquiring their objective. It is unclear when this will occur; in MY opinion, it will be at the start of the seven years called the TRIBULATION. What is very clear to me is *THAT IT WILL OCCUR.* I see from news reports of the alliances already taking place between those countries and the events of the day moving in that direction, in spite of all the efforts of PEOPLE to try stop or change the circumstances.

The powerful growth of the European community and its military force (NATO), protectionist treaties between Russia and Persia (Iran) and others plus the gradual but perceptible disillusionment of the United States of America with Israel were ALL prophesied hundreds of years ago. That does not even take into account the outright hostility of some of the members of the European community toward Israel.

Daniel, another prophet of the exile, tells in his book, chapter eleven (11) verses thirty-six through verse forty-five (45) of the rise and few of the actions of the ruler during the TRIBULATION called the Anti-Christ. There are some with much more education than myself that claim these verses only refer to a king of Persia by the name of Antiochus Epiphanes. I grant this king did what is described in these verses; however, IF these verses referred only to him, WHY DID JESUS MENTION these exact verses over four hundred years later?

Daniel in the seventh chapter verses nine and ten tells of the coming judgment of the ungodly. (9) "I kept looking until thrones were set up and the Ancient of Days took HIS seat; HIS vesture was like white snow and the hair of HIS head like pure wool. HIS throne was ablaze, its wheels were a burning fire. (10) A river of fire was flowing and coming out from before HIM; Thousands upon thousands were attending HIM, and myriads upon myriads were standing before HIM; the court sat, and the books were opened." This appears to be the same that is mentioned in the Book of Revelation, chapter twenty, verses ten through fifteen, known as the White Throne Judgment.

In MY interpretation of these two verses, I see first thrones, more than one, but the ANCIENT of DAYS, GOD, HE that has no beginning and has no end takes HIS seat on ONE throne. HIS appearance indicates purity. Many thousands are there to attend to HIM and the proceedings. Fire is the symbol but also a method of cleansing. The perhaps millions standing before HIM are there to be JUDGED for what they did or did not do in their lifetime. More of this scripture will be mentioned near or at the end of this document.

Micah prophesied the complete destruction of Jerusalem and the Temple.

"Therefore, on account of you Zion will be plowed as a field, Jerusalem will become a heap of ruins, and the mountain of the Temple will become high places of the forest" (MICAH 3:1 NAS). THIS did occur in seventy

A.D. when the Roman army destroyed Jerusalem and the Temple, over four hundred years later.

HE begins in chapter four with the events AFTER the Tribulation period, how Israel will be the focus of *ALL* the nations. The last verses, nine through thirteen, speak of the trouble and pain THEY must endure to have the previous blessings. Chapter five, verses four through fifteen tell of the second coming of their Messiah, Jesus Christ, the ONLY SON of GOD.

Zephaniah speaks in his book, in the third chapter, verse eight.

"Therefore wait for me," declares the LORD, "for the day when I rise up as a witness. Indeed, MY decision is to gather nations, to assemble kingdoms, to pour out on them MY indignation. ALL MY burning anger; For all the earth will be devoured by the FIRE of MY zeal."

This WILL happen at the end of the Tribulation period but also may be also indicating the event at the end of the Millennium.

Just as an added note: the first destruction of the world was by water, the second will be by FIRE!

Zechariah will be the next and the last of the Old Testament prophets mentioned. I mentioned before there will be a time when The United States will turn its back, goodbye, on the Nation of Israel.

"It will come about in that day that I will make Jerusalem a heavy stone for *ALL* peoples; *ALL* who lift it will be severely injured. And *ALL* the nations of the earth *WILL* be gathered against it"(ZECHARIAH 12:3 NAS). The italics are mine to emphasis that we in the United States (ALL peoples, ALL who lift it, ALL nations) will be included.

In chapter fourteen (14) and the first eleven (11) verses tells of the second coming of the LORD JESUS and the results of HIS arrival.

The above was given as a very short *historical* overview of the "Old Testament". Each prophet, every person mentioned said "goodbye" in one fashion or another, maybe not verbally but a goodbye none the less. There are as many different ways and types of goodbyes almost as there are people. Remember they are the way "I" imagine them; they ARE MY OPINION.

So that you may think but all is NOT all doom and gloom:

"It will come about after this that I will pour out MY SPIRIT on all mankind and your sons and daughters will prophesy, your old men will dream dreams, your young men will see visions" (JOEL 2:28 NAS).

AND, "He will restore the hearts of the fathers to their children and the hearts of the children to their fathers, so that I will NOT come and smite the land with a curse" (MALACHI 4:6 NAS).

Now I will begin the final events which WILL lead up to "THE FINAL FAREWELL."

As I begin in the NEW TESTAMENT, I will begin with the first four books, called the FOUR GOSPELS. In the FOUR GOSPELS, there are some incidents that are repeated. If there is a repeat, I will possibly quote one and refer to the others simply as where they are located. Two of the gospels are from "eyewitnesses" and two are the words from an "eyewitness".

Please remember eyewitness accounts of ANY incident may vary depending on any number of factors, i.e. the location of the individual at the time, was the person in front, back, off to one side, close or far away. It could be affected by the time of day, the age of the person, their experiences, the length of time between the incident and the report or even their gender. If a modern-day police report is read from four individuals concerning an accident or incident, you could almost believe each was witness to an entirely different incident.

It is amazing all the incidents in the FOUR GOSPELS are remarkably consistent with only slight variations, none of which change the overall picture of the incident, mostly only in a few of the words that were said. Many of the minor differences can be attributed to the translation of the Greek word into English. The Greek word, like English words, may have several similar interpretations, but all of them mean generally the same.

Although the actual word "goodbye" was not spoken, as such, JESUS said it, several times, in several different ways. Jesus spoke to two different groups of people. Both groups exist to this day: believers and unbelievers. To the "BELIEVERS", HE in the modern way of speaking, "I am leaving but I'LL see you later'. To the unbeliever, "Goodbye, you will not WANT to see me again," or with much sadness because the person refused to change. How did HE say these things, let me explain first to the UNBELIEVER.

Jesus had arrived in the country of the Gerasenes. HE was met by a man who lived among the tombs and possessed with demons. Jesus demanded the demons to leave the man. For HE had been saying to him, 'Come out of the man, you unclean spirit!'" (MARK 5:19, LUKE 8:39 NAS).

Notice the forceful demand of "get out and be gone!" The demons, literally hundreds of them, realized this and begged Jesus NOT to send them the abyss before their time and asked that they could inhabit a herd of swine close by. (Swine to the Jew was an unclean animal.) Jesus gave them permission to do exactly that and they left the man and into the swine. The swine went crazy and ran into the sea and were drowned. This incident was reported to the townspeople by the keepers of the swine, who then asked Jesus to LEAVE and implied "don't come back." This has been a mystery to me as to why they would be so objectionable. The only reason I have read or heard is that the town was engaged in an occupation strictly forbidden in the Law of Moses, the raising and possibly the eating of swine, an unclean animal.

There was a rich man and he asked Jesus what he needed to do to inherit eternal life. After determining the rich man had complied with everything according to the LAW, given by Moses, Jesus told him the one thing he lacked was to sell all his possessions and to give ALL to the poor and follow HIM. The rich man left, with an extremely sad goodbye, unable to GIVE UP his treasures on earth.

> "And Jesus looking around, said to HIS disciples, "How hard it will be for those who are wealthy to enter the Kingdom of GOD!" (MARK 10:23, MATTHEW 19:23, LUKE 18:24 NAS).

I can only imagine the pain my LORD had as HE watched the man walk away and perhaps whispered to HIMSELF goodbye and to know that the man was so very close to eternal life but chose instead eternal death.

Another example is in the parable of the ten virgins. In this parable there were ten virgins awaiting the arrival of the bridegroom. Five of them had oil for their lamps and five did not. The bridegroom suddenly arrived at midnight. The five without the oil for their lamps wanted some of the oil from the other five; however, they said "NO" that if they gave them oil there may not be enough to light the way; So the five "foolish virgins" hurried away to find someone to sell them some oil. The five virgins with oil and the bridegroom entered into the bridal chamber and the door was locked. When the foolish virgins arrived, they knocked on the door to gain entry. Without stating all the various lessons to be learned from this parable (MATTHEW 25:1-13), I will only state that those that are NOT ready for the return of Jesus and believe because they are good people will find too late that JESUS may say, "Go away! I do not know who you are. GOODBYE!"

In the previous mentioned incidents except for the first there is a possibility of change and therefore perhaps HE may see them again. All three were only illustrated to show the finality of the conversation at the time. Now it will be illustrated the difference in the conversation to BELIEVERS.

The first is actually the same scriptures involving the demons above. The demons had been removed from the man in the tombs and the swine had run into the sea and drowned. The man, from whom the demons had been removed, had asked Jesus to allow him, now in his right mind and cured, to go with and follow HIM.

> "And HE did not let him but HE said to him, Go home to your people and report to them what great things the LORD has done for you, and how HE had mercy on you" (MARK 5:19, Luke 8:39 NAS).

The compassion for the man is very evident in the words spoken; it was a gentle "goodbye, see you later". Jesus knew the man could be better testimony for the Kingdom of GOD among his friends and relatives because they KNEW of his previous condition and could see for themselves the glorious work of GOD.

Jesus had finished feeding five thousand "men", not included in this number were the wives and children, with five loaves of bread and two fish.

> "Immediately Jesus made HIS disciples get into the boat and go ahead of HIM to the other side to Bethsaida, while HE HIMSELF was sending the crowd away... After bidding the farewell to the crowd, HE left for the mountain to pray." (MARK 6:45-46, Matthew 14:22-23 NAS).

When Jesus said "see you later" to HIS disciples, as far as they were concerned, it was with HIS intention of meeting them again at Bethsaida. It would be only a temporary separation BUT does not appear, at least to me, they thought of how HE might get there. They had taken, apparently, the only boat available.

How, you may ask, did Jesus meet them in Bethsaida when there was no boat available? As you read the following scriptures, Jesus found them, halfway across the Sea of Galilee, rowing hard against the wind and HE (Jesus) was walking on the water. As soon as HE got into the boat, they were immediately on the shore.

Another time, Jesus had fed four thousand, in addition to women and children, with seven loaves of bread and a few small fishes, before again getting into a boat to travel to Dalmanutha. HE sent the crowd away with perhaps the word of "Shalom" (Peace). The Bible only states HE sent them away, but in my heart I can only believe it HAD to be with words of peace and comfort.

Jesus now begins to tell HIS disciples the method of HIS departure. HE informs them in advance, in an effort for them to understand the type of departure AND it would only be a temporary separation.

> "For HE was teaching HIS disciples and telling them, "The Son of Man is to be delivered into the hands of men, and they will kill HIM; and when HE has been killed, HE will rise three days later" (MARK 9:31, Matthew 17:22-23, LUKE 9:44 NAS).

Unfortunately, according to the next verse they did not understand and what is more astounding to me is they were AFRAID to ask. Here were several strong men used to the rough life of fishermen and were AFRAID to ask the man, they followed, a question about HIS leaving them!

This next indication of goodbye from Jesus occurs just prior to HIS actual crucifixion, as HE and HIS disciples were eating the PASSOVER meal.

> "Truly I say to you, I will never again drink of the fruit of the vine until that day when I drink it new, in the kingdom of GOD" (MARK 14:25, MATTHEW 26:29, LUKE 22:18 NAS).

This was a clear indication of HE was about to leave them. Wine was the staple at every meal at this time in history and was consumed by all the people from their earliest days until the death.

Wine was so much a staple it is used in the procedure of circumcision of an eight-DAY-old boy. A drop of wine is placed in the mouth of the boy. I may also add, this is WINE, not grape juice.

The last recorded goodbye was AFTER HIS death and resurrection. Jesus met with HIS disciples and had explained, I believe, the reasons for what happened previously. "And HE said to them, 'Go into the all world and preach the gospel to all creation.'" This was only a temporary separation. ALL of them KNEW HE was to return to establish a NEW and different Kingdom. This is evident in the recorded activities of the disciples, except for few and rare times, THEY DID NOT LEAVE JERSUSALEM. They fully expected Jesus to return very shortly to Jerusalem and do away with the Roman occupation and begin the new and everlasting kingdom. That was two thousand years ago. What they did not know or understand was the GOSPEL would be delivered to the Gentiles first and then entire world would have the opportunity to accept or reject it.

I mentioned briefly the acts of some apostles when they HAD to say goodbye. I will now attempt to give specific times involved.

Before I continue, I must state a fact; THERE was no GOSPEL before the resurrection of Jesus. The GOSPEL; IS the death, burial and RESURRECTION of Jesus, the MESSIAH! Without ALL three of these events, the GOSPEL would NOT exist and everyone would die in their sins. I state this because from this point until JESUS RETURNS, all events, prophesies and actions revolve around the true and only GOSPEL, the death, burial and resurrection of Jesus.

The apostles and everyone who believes in the resurrected CHRIST is required to spread the word of the Gospel to as many and as often as possible (ACTS CHAPTER 3 and 4). This was what Peter and John were doing as they entered the temple. At the gate of the temple was a man, begging for alms, who had been lame from birth. Instead of giving the man alms, they healed him in the "Name of Jesus". Because of the testimony and healing in the "Name of Jesus", the hierarchy of the JEWS were infuriated. The JEWS had them thrown in prison. Because it was evening, it was the next morning when they, along with the man who was healed, were brought before the council of JEWS. After discussion, they were told NOT to speak in the name of Jesus again.

"But Peter and John answered and said to them, "Whether it is right in the sight of GOD to give heed to you rather than GOD, you be the judge; for we cannot stop speaking about what we have seen and heard" (ACTS 419-20 NAS).

Basically, in modern terms, Peter and John was saying, "We are not going to stop so see you around."

Stephen was designated to help in the service of the apostles. He was charged by the "Jews" as a disrupter and although there were many witnessed against him nothing could be "proven" which was worthy of death, and death is what they wanted to inflict. False witnesses were obtained, and Stephen was given the chance to refute the charges.

Stephen, in his rebuttal of the charges against him, reviewed the history of the Jewish people and all was well and it was reported he had the "face of an angel" as he spoke. Perhaps his face glowed with the glory of GOD.

"And fixing their gaze on him, all who were sitting in the Council saw his face like the face of an angel" (ACTS 6:15 NAS). It appears this fact had little to no effect on them.

They listened to Stephen until he accused them (their forefathers) of killing the prophets and said, "You received the LAW as ordained by angels, and yet did not keep it" (ACTS 7:53 NAS).

Those listening immediately began to shout and gnash their teeth and throw stones at him.

The last words of Stephen of goodbye as he was dying was, "Then falling on his knees, he cried out with a loud voice, LORD, do not hold this sin against them!" Having said this, he fell asleep" (died) (ACTS 7:60 NAS). Even as he died, Stephen was saying goodbye and was forgiving them at the same time.

Phillip "the evangelist" was sent by "an angel of the LORD" to meet with a eunuch from the Ethiopia, from the court of Queen Candance, traveling from Jerusalem back to Ethiopia. Upon explaining to the eunuch the scriptures he "happened" to be reading, the eunuch believed in Jesus as the Messiah and wanted to be baptized as a profession of that faith. Upon rising from the water, Phillip was whisked away by the HOLY SPIRIT and the eunuch went happily on his way to Ethiopia as if it was a normal occurrence for a person to suddenly disappear. The fact that his sins were forgiven let him know that it was not a permanent goodbye but only a temporary separation for the two of them.

The next goodbye involved a severe persecutor of the followers of Jesus (they were not called Christians, yet). His name was Saul, later changed to Paul. Saul was on his way to Damascus with letters to bring the followers back to Jerusalem for trial and imprisonment. This implies to me they were judged to be guilty unless proven innocent. Even ROMAN Law, at the time, required witnesses and a trial before a judge.

The life of Saul (Paul) was changed radically when he met with Jesus on the road to Damascus. His zeal for the Jewish religion was turned into zeal for Jesus. His conversion was so radical, the Jews in Damascus plotted to kill him. The plot was discovered, and with the gates of the city guarded by those wishing to kill him, "the followers" of Jesus let him escape by letting him down through a window in a basket. As he left, I believe those allowing him to escape must have said something on the order of, "Goodbye and GOD be with you." Or may have said the prayer given to Aaron by GOD many hundreds of years before: "The LORD bless you; The LORD make HIS face shine upon you; And be gracious to you; The LORD lift up His countenance on you and give you peace."

In Jerusalem, the arguments with a group of Jews called "the Hellenistic Jews" became such that again there was a plot to kill him. The brethren in Jerusalem sent him away to Tarsus via Caesarea in order to restore peace. Is it possible Saul was too argumentative? The reason I say this is the next verse following states, "So the church throughout all Judea and Galilee and Samaria enjoyed peace, being built up; and going on in the fear of the LORD and in the comfort of the HOLY SPIRIT, it continued to increase" (ACTS 9:31 NAS).

So was Saul leaving, one of relief, or was it just to prevent him from being killed or maybe a little of both? I have had the experience of when an individual departed my home and I said goodbye it was with a huge sigh of relief from my wife AND myself! We had a great affection for the individual, and since my wife has died many years ago, I still do. It just happened there was something irritating him this time and he, rather than suppress the feelings while in our home, took it out on the things in our home. I will add, he knew better than to try to take out his frustration on my wife or myself; he may have ended up with a broken jaw or worse.

In the following, from the Book of ACTS and until the Book of Revelation, Paul (Saul) traveled throughout the Gentile countryside preaching the NEW GOSPEL! He had, I am sure, told many people, numerous times farewell, but it was only a temporary parting. He would return, until on his way to Jerusalem, he was at Caesarea, in the home of Phillip, the evangelist. While there, apparently the four daughters of Phillip and a prophet from Jerusalem prophesied the imprisonment and perhaps the death of Paul. They tried to convince Paul not to go with much pleading and tears.

> "Then Paul answered, 'What mean ye to weep and to break mine heart? For I am ready not to be bound only, but also to die at Jerusalem for the name of the LORD JESUS'" (ACTS 21:13 KJV).

This was not only a heartbreaking goodbye for those there at the time but also for Paul.

Paul did continue to Jerusalem, and as prophesied, he was arrested by the leaders of the Jews and only through the intervention of the Roman guards escaped from being beat to death. Under Roman jurisdiction and because another plot to kill Paul was discovered, Paul was transferred to Caesarea and under the jurisdiction of Governor Felix. After at least two years in a Roman prison, Paul was placed on a prison ship bound for Rome.

From my understanding of this type of ship, as it began to sail, the prisoners were in the hold (bottom) of the ship, with no visible access to watch their country disappear from sight. How sad it must have been to say goodbye, not able to look upon and know they would NEVER again see their homeland.

Paul, in his writings to the various churches and individuals, with the exception of the Book of Romans, said farewell in the almost exactly the same way, "Grace to you."

I wrote all the above to indicate the various ways people say goodbye to others. I will now begin, as this part of the equation indicates, the reasons for and then "The Final Farewell."

I MUST begin with GOD is a merciful, loving and patient GOD. HE has been "dealing" with people for six thousand years. People, generally, have caused HIM grief, pain and HE even had to turn HIS back of HIS chosen ones. Over the years HE attempted to "straighten" out those without interfering with their RIGHT to freedom of choice. The people chose to worship the "creation instead of the CREATOR". As a last attempt, GOD sent HIS son to earth in the form of a normal man, to live, preach the coming of the Kingdom, to be condemned, executed like a criminal, be buried and after three days rise from the dead. This *IS* the ultimate sacrifice for the sins of the world, for *ALL* those who would believe.

> "For the wages of sin is death, but the gift of GOD is eternal
> life in Christ Jesus our LORD" (ROMANS 6:23 NAS).

Before I continue, I will state, a person EARNS eternal death, there is an effort expended, thus wages of sin, however eternal LIFE is a GIFT! A gift is something you are given FREELY without any effort on the part of the person. As with any gift the person MUST accept it before it becomes his own.

GOD did NOT "spring" this upon an unsuspecting world. Beginning with the eviction of Adam and Eve from the Garden of Eden, GOD began to warn people of the upcoming disasters and how to avoid being swept into an eternal death. GOD even went so far as to WRITE all the predictions and consequences in a BOOK, the Bible, for everyone to read and UNDERSTAND.

Eternal death? That is the total separation from the Love and Grace of the Father, GOD, and the continuous and forever torment and pain of Hell. It is something GOD wants NO ONE to have to endure; however, HE will NOT interfere with the right of choice. IF anyone will spend an eternity in Hell, it will by their own choice.

How did HE warn of the upcoming events which will occur? God began in the Garden of Eden when HE told the serpent, Satan in the form of the snake, that although he may bite the heel of the Savior, the Savior would CRUSH the head of the serpent (Satan). After many years of warnings of a coming disaster, HE had Noah begin to build an Ark and still waited one hundred years before executing judgment. The ARK could have been made by GOD in a moment of time, but HE allowed time to pass in an effort that no one would PERISH! All were destroyed EXCEPT eight, who took refuge in an Ark filled with animals.

With the total destruction of humans still in their minds, was anything really learned? It does not seem so because as the population grew AGAIN, and although GOD, apparently, spoke directly to them, HIS voice was ignored when told to populate the entire world. They all gathered into one area and began to build a tower to reach into Heaven? GOD had to intervene AGAIN by confusing their language in order to disperse the people to all the parts of the world.

It was many years before GOD chose again one man this time to become a "Father of Nations". Abraham was to begin a new and different race of people. Directed to even a new country, Abraham, through his wife Sarah, began the plan of GOD. GOD had told Abraham the very land he, Abraham, walked upon would be given to his descendants; it was "The Promised Land".

Through much hardship, including four hundred years of separation from the land and slavery, it was time for the nation of Israel to assume possession of the "Promised Land" and be the NEW race of people for GOD. The people were given Laws and Rules in which to live and also the consequences for not following them. The people rebelled and had to be led through the desert for forty Years by Moses to eliminate a rebellious faction of the people. They were FINALLY ready to enter and possess the land promised to Abraham hundreds of years before.

After the death of the leaders and elders; those who had fought the inhabitants and overcame obstacles to obtain the land, rebellion once more began to taint the population. For the next three hundred years, because of recurring rebellion, men and women were raised to judge the people and defeat the enemies placed to rule over them. There would be peace while the judge was alive; however, almost as soon as the Judge died, rebellion began and the process would begin again.

"They did not destroy the nations, concerning whom the LORD commanded them; But were mingled among the heathen, and learned their works. And served their idols; which were a snare unto them. Yea, they sacrificed their sons and daughters unto devils" (PSALMS 106:34-37 KJV).

The last judge and first prophet of GOD, Samuel, when asked by the people to anoint a king over them, objected. GOD spoke to Samuel and told him they were not rejecting him, Samuel, but GOD to rule over them. Samuel prophesied what would take place IF they had a king rule over them; however, the people "insisted" they wanted a king, so reluctantly, Samuel anointed for them a king.

With a king ruling, it was now the "Age of the Prophets". Prophets would forecast coming events along with requests for repentance for the evil deeds the population. The prophets told of events which happened in their lifetime but also future events that would happen, two to three thousand years later.

There are "Prophets of GOD", false prophets and those that prophesy. I must explain the difference between the three.

A "Prophet of GOD" is a person who, when speaking, speaks with the authority and unction of GOD. Every forecasted event will occur EXACTLY, in every detail as predicted. A false prophet may be right at times, however, is NOT one hundred percent correct, one hundred percent of the time. If there is an error, no matter how slight, that person is a FALSE PROPHET! A person who prophesies is anyone who speaks the word of GOD but not necessarily in the form of events in the future. In our "modern" times it is one who has accepted Jesus as the Son of GOD, who believes with all their heart that Jesus died, was buried and rose again on the third day to become his sacrifice for their sins. Each person when they speak of the LOVE of the Father and Jesus, when they quote a verse from the Bible or tell another of the GRACE of GOD, every believer of JESUS and GOD, prophesies.

There is an adversary who strives to usurp the throne of GOD and has been waging a war for that purpose since the creation of the world. The war and the various battles for supremacy have been raging for the HEARTS and MINDS of people for four thousand years. One of the tactics employed is to attempt to prevent prophesies of GOD or those who prophesy about the LOVE of GOD from occurring, which to my feeble mind is an effort in futility.

The people I know would not believe the difficulties I have had to write this and the two books before. ONLY through a constant "CHASING" the demons out of my presence and the will of GOD have I been able to write anything at all. "Greater is HE that is with us than those of whom is without"(paraphrased).

The adversary has even attempted to prevent *"THE* PROPHESIES" concerning the coming of JESUS and HIS ultimate sacrifice. God in a final demonstration of HIS love provided, a choice, to accept or reject this sacrifice of HIS Son. The choice is always for the individual; GOD gave everyone the right to choose. The adversary, the Devil, will make every attempt to make and keep that CHOICE from the individual.

I now approach the final prophesy, written in the Bible. John, while imprisoned on the Isle of Patmos, had a vision from Jesus concerning future events, many of which are still to occur. It is NOT my intention nor the theme of this document to provide details of that prophesy. The interpretations of the Book of Revelation have been told and written about since it was first presented to the churches, two thousand years ago. I will provide only a brief description of the events that lead up to the "Final Farewell".

I have, for my benefit and study, divided the Book of Revelation into five sections. They are (one) the churches, (two) warnings, (three) judgments, (four) parenthetical and (five) the Millennium. I will attempt to give a brief summary of each section without a lot of detail and interpretation; interpret only to clarify a point. The interpretations most needed at this time are: When speaking of "the dragon", it is symbolic of Satan. When "the beast" with ten horns is mentioned, it is symbolic of the anti-Christ, and a "beast" with two horns is symbolic of the false prophet.

There are seven churches listed. Upon examination, each is the condition not only various churches of today but also the past, plus if so applied honestly is also the condition of the individual or even a nation.

They speak of the condition, how to remove or solve the condition and what is the result *IF* repentance of the condition is not taken. For the individual, although it could easily be taken as to apply to churches only, upon close examination will show how a person may think under certain conditions and general overall behavior. Thus it is easy to see how they can apply to a person as well. A church or individual can and must change; it is more difficult for a nation to do so because often a nation is under the control of our adversary, Satan.

Study carefully the seven churches of the Book of Revelation. Make the necessary changes to conform to the life for which Jesus died. Each carries with it the reward for change, and although the reward is fantastic, it is only a reward. The greatest result is *ETERNAL LIFE.*

The next section is what I call the WARNINGS. It is actually the largest section the Book of Revelation. It is so because GOD is a GOD of MERCY and LOVE; He wishes ALL will come to accept HIM and live in fellowship with HIM and none should PERISH. Twenty-one warnings are issued; each subsection, of which are three, becomes more severe than the previous. It appears, with each rejection of the warning, the anger of GOD has an increase of temperature. As each section is written, it may be interrupted by a section of parenthetical.

The subsections I refer to are called: seals, trumpets and bowls. As I continue it will become evident why I refer to them this way.

First are the seals; there are seven seals on a scroll. As each is removed from the scroll, a different scene is exposed. The first four seals are commonly referred to as the four horsemen of the Apocalypse. There are many who have attempted to describe this first horseman. I will not, except to say it is a coming ruler, be it be a person or nation or whatever, all agree it will be a ruler of some kind. The next three indicate extreme inflation, disease and death. The second takes peace from the earth and I assume there will be much chaos. The third horseman brings with it extreme inflation. It will take a day's wages to buy a day of food. The fourth horseman, Death, causes one fourth of those on the earth to be killed; that is approximately one point five billion people of the present population of six billion. Everything I have read from others appears to agree on these points. To read about them, there is very little reason NOT to SEE it is exactly that. In my opinion, it is at this time the Rapture *COULD* take place. Please note I said COULD not will. I say this because out of one point five billion, as many as two hundred million Christians could disappear and not even be missed.

From this point until the end of this BOOK there are as many opinions as there are people. I will only attempt the say what the Bible says without very much elaboration or interpretation.

The next three seals are different from one to another but tell of three distinct and different things. The first of the three or the fifth seal tells about the people, as they appear in the throne room, they were killed, or slain, for the word of GOD. This multitude of individuals are from the past but will be joined by more to arrive from the future; the future, POSSIBLY, being during the remaining years of the tribulation.

The sixth seal indicates what can happen when GOD is only angry. It has been described by "learned" individuals that it appears to be a nuclear exchange between countries. That may well be and the description of the sky "rolling" back does fit. If that is a fact, why according to verses fifteen through seventeen, do everyone attempt to hide from the "wrath" of the Lamb (GOD). Of course, it could be said people are trying to avoid the fallout from nuclear explosions; that is NOT what the verse says. It does say "from the Wrath of GOD".

Chapter seven begins with a parenthetical. It tells of the sealing of a hundred forty-four thousand Jewish evangelicals and the arrival of a multitude of individuals from every nation and tongue. It is a hundred forty-four thousand Jewish individuals turned loose upon the earth to preach Jesus and HIS sacrifice and the arrival of the multitude COULD possibly be what is called the RAPTURE of present-day Christians? The Bible is silent on the subject of why and nothing is said as to when they did or may occur. A *parenthetical* can occur at any time before mentioned events, during or at some time in the future. I will only say they will occur, therefore "be ready" the timing is solely in the mind of GOD!

> The last seal, the seventh, "in my opinion" is the calm *before the storm*. It simply states *"there was silence in heaven for about half an hour"* (REVELATION 8:1 NAS).

Chapter eight continues after the time of silence with, of what I term the building anger of GOD, the seven trumpets. There are differences of opinion as to whether each event quickly follows another or there is a space of time between each. *IN MY OPINION*, there is a space of time. I say this because when GOD dealt with Pharaoh in the Book of Exodus for the release of the Hebrews, there was a space of time, enough to allow Pharaoh a chance to repent. It is my belief GOD, as the merciful GOD HE is, will give the unbelieving world a chance to repent; however, I will also say, it is HIS choice.

The first four trumpets, when they sound they place in turmoil nature and the very things people need to live and survive. Plants, one-third are destroyed, one-third of everything in the seas are destroyed, one-third of the streams and rivers are made useless and even one-third of life giving sunlight is withdrawn, which, I may add, would affect the growth of plants necessary for life.

It is apparent to me there will be a HUGE shortage of food and fresh water with devastating effect on every living animal and human on the earth. The inflationary cost of basic commodities will soar; only the rich and powerful will be able to live in any relative comfort. The unrest and turmoil of the "common" person will increase substantially.

Trumpet number five is designed strictly to torment people. Out of the depths of, I will say, Hell, comes strange appearing things called in the Bible locusts. From the description, they are very strange indeed, unlike any locust I have ever seen, and they do nothing like any locust I know. They only live for five months, which certain species do, but during this time, they don't eat any green thing, something a locust would normally do. The only thing they do is torment people by stinging them with the force of a scorpion. As an added torment, although the stings will be so terrifically painful, people will beg to die, NO ONE will be able to die. I cannot imagine, there will be NOT one funeral for five months!

Now we have to add to the turmoil of finding food to eat and even water to drink, the pain of the sting from this locust.

When the sixth angel sounds his trumpet, there will be a gathering of armies, two hundred million, and one-third of mankind will be killed. From the number of the population remaining, it would still equal to over a "billion" people. It appears as though these armies may arrive from four different directions or perhaps four different countries, whichever, they will be brought together by four fallen angels.

As these armies gather, one-third of the population will be killed, apparently, in my opinion, by the armies as they advance on their objective, still no one repents of their sins.

Chapter ten and eleven are again parenthetical chapters. Chapter ten states, a strong angel comes from Heaven with a little book. The little book is given to John for him to eat, which he when he does eat it, he is told he would again be prophesying to many people and "kings". To explain "the little book", it is the word of GOD and when he prophesies, GOD's word will come forth from within him.

Chapter eleven tells about measuring the Temple and Altar of GOD and then immediately "two witnesses" appear in Jerusalem. There are many "ideas" about who or what these two witnesses may be. They range from Moses and Elisha to the Jewish and Christian churches. IN MY OPINION, although I have no knowledge of who the two might be, I believe them to be actual, resurrected men. My reason is simple: after their work is complete, they are ALLOWED by GOD to be killed by the anti-Christ. Their "bodies" will lay in the streets of Jerusalem for three and a half days and be observed by the EN-

TIRE world, which will be rejoicing and having parties because they ARE dead. NOTE: For the entire world will be able to observe their bodies, which was not possible until very recently. NOW, any event can be seen throughout the entire world via satellites, INSTANTLY, as it happens.

To the horror of the WORLD, after three and half days, the two witnesses are still laying dead in the street. There is a voice HEARD, "Come up here" and the two witnesses will suddenly become alive and are taken into Heaven.

The eleventh chapter ends with the seventh trumpet sounding, announcing the kingdoms of the world are now the kingdom of GOD. The "WRATH of GOD" is about to be executed.

Chapters twelve, thirteen and fourteen are parenthetical chapters. A brief summary of these chapters follows: Chapter twelve states symbolically about the birth and escape from Satan of Jesus and then about a war in Heaven. Satan and one-third of the angels are removed from access to Heaven and because Satan knows time is short starts havoc on earth. Satan begins an all-out persecution of any and all believers of GOD through its agents, the anti-Christ and the false prophet (chapter thirteen). As part of the persecution, a number is given to ALL unbelievers, so anyone without the number can be identified. Food and anything needed to live can be withheld or the person could be killed outright (chapter fourteen). The chapter ends with the announcement; the wrath of GOD is about to begin.

Chapter fifteen is about the seven bowls filled with the plagues and The WRATH of GOD!

Chapter sixteen: The first bowl is poured; a loathsome and malignant sore appears on everyone that has the mark, number or the name of the anti-Christ on them. Bowl two: as the bowl is poured on the sea, it became as if it were blood and EVERY living thing in the sea dies. It has been said by some, the sea mentioned refers ONLY to the Mediterranean Sea, but in my opinion, that would not be in keeping with the Wrath of GOD; ALL seas will be affected. Bowl three: the bowl is poured upon the rivers and streams and they became like blood, undrinkable. Bowl four: this bowl is poured upon the sun and the heat becomes intensified to the point of scorching everyone on earth. In spite of these things, people only blasphemed GOD and refused to repent. Bowl five is poured out upon the seat of the anti-Christ and it becomes so dark that it causes pain. They still refuse to repent.

What a world it will be! Everyone covered with sores, the availability of food scarce, any food being transported across the seas has ceased and other modes of transport, no doubt, slowed to an almost stop, life giving water has become nearly undrinkable and the unbearable heat.

I have been in some very dark places in my life, but never in a place so dark that it caused pain. Pain may have been from stubbing my toe but not to the point of gnawing my tongue.

Bowl number six is different from the previous five. This bowl is poured upon the River Euphrates. The river becomes completely dry to provide a way for "Kings of the East". There is a gathering of armies and it is unclear to me if it is part of the armies already mentioned or the "kings of the east" are additional to them. The one thing that is very clear: they are gathering for a war against GOD, which will take place IN ONE DAY. They are being gathered to a place called in Hebrew, Har-Magedon, translated, Mountain of Megiddo or in English, it is well known to many as Armageddon.

Armageddon is well known by believers and unbelievers alike as the ultimate "time" of destruction, but in actuality it is a *PLACE* of gathering for the final battle for supremacy of the world. The world has NEVER witnessed true Armageddon.

Chapter sixteen ends with the seventh bowl being poured out and the announcement by the angel: "It is done." The last of the bowls of Wrath is being poured out. The result is an earthquake more intense than anything ever witnessed before. The great city is split into three parts. There are differences of opinion as what city it would be: Rome, Babylon or Jerusalem. I have no opinion except to say it must be a city closely involved, at that time, with the anti-Christ because, in addition, all cities of the nations also crumble. Every island disappears and all the mountains are leveled. I can only say it is an earthquake I would NOT ever want to experience. The only one I have ever experienced rattled the building for a short time and things on shelves or loose on a table fell to the floor. THAT WAS VERY SUFFICENT for me.

Next, "huge hailstones" weighing a hundred pounds come down from "Heaven". Do people repent? Not at all, they only continue to blaspheme GOD for the hail.

The first sentence in Psalm 14:1 states: "The fool has said in his heart, 'There is no GOD'" (NAS). I am told the actual translation from Hebrew says:

"The fool says in his heart, NO to GOD." In either case "there is no GOD" or "no to GOD", the people living during the before mentioned TIMES are quite the FOOL!

As a personal note: In 1958, I was in Nebraska and read an accident report concerning an aircraft encountering hailstones. A Locheed Constellation, considered, at the time, the "Queen of the skies", one of the best built, most luxurious aircraft at that time, flew into a thunderstorm, apparently with full confidence the aircraft was so well built it would be perfectly safe. It encountered hailstones, estimated to be the size of golf balls, perhaps weighing as much as three to four OUNCES each. The aircraft was so severely damaged, there were huge holes in the wings and fuselage, windows smashed and broken; it was barely flyable and had to make an emergency landing at the nearest airport. Damage was so extensive, the aircraft could not be repaired enough to ever fly again and had to be completely destroyed. If such damage could happen to one of the best aircraft in the skies at that time from four-ounce hailstones, I can only imagine the damage from a hundred pound hailstone.

Chapter seventeen, a parenthetical, begins with an angel showing John a woman clothed in scarlet and purple, symbol of royalty, and all kinds of precious gems and jewels. She is sitting on a scarlet beast, a symbol of the anti-Christ. This is the false religion of the anti-Christ and has the false prophet as its leader. What is seen must have been a fabulous sight because John has a sense of wonder about the vision.

The attending angel brings John back to "reality" as it explains the vision. The woman is the false religion of the anti-Christ. The inhabitants of earth follow the false religion and the anti-Christ believing he must be a god. The anti-Christ wages a war against "The Lamb", Jesus, but does NOT succeed.

The woman sits on seven mountains; many have interpreted this to be ROME, because Rome was built on seven hills. I will only say it, a city, becomes the center of the false religion. The description of the seven heads and ten horns of the beast are seven kingdoms from the past which form the foundation of the last kingdom and ten horns, "kings", that GIVE their power to the anti-Christ, but not before three are overcome. The irony is the woman is destroyed because apparently of jealousy of her wealth (gems and jewels), prestige and apparent power. The chapter ends with the explanation that the woman, a symbolic of the religion and the city which is the center of that religion, is destroyed by the anti-Christ and the ten "kings".

Chapter eighteen speaks of the fall of the religious entity and the apparent rejoicing in heaven but the mourning of those on earth. It states destruction happens in ONE day and all the merchants and those who were made wealthy by the existence of the religion and city remained well clear of the burning of the city. I have read, this is because the city will be destroyed by a nuclear explosion. The chapter ends with the acclamation of the angels of the destruction and how it was justified.

Chapter nineteen: This chapter is in three sections. The first is the marriage of the Lamb, Jesus, to HIS bride, the church and the rejoicing of the marriage. Sections two and three are the return of Jesus with HIS army and the very short but total destruction of the armies gathered against HIM. The anti-Christ and the false prophet, ONLY, are seized and thrown ALIVE into the Lake of Fire and the armies assembled are killed and birds are called to feast on their bodies.

Chapter twenty begins with the seizing of Satan and being thrown into a bottomless pit and held there for a thousand years. Next is the judgment of those killed during the tribulation for the word of Christ. These are given their place in the kingdom along with the BRIDE of Christ who was already with Christ. The FIRST resurrection does NOT to occur for a thousand years.

There is a thousand years of PEACE and TRANQUILLITY before Satan is once more released into the world. Strange as it seems, in spite of a thousand years of PEACE and Jesus providing all the needs of the people, there is a rebellion, AGAIN!

The logical question at this time may be, "If there has been perfect peace for a thousand years, why would GOD again release Satan to deceive people and cause a rebellion?" The reason began with Adam in the Garden of Eden. GOD has given every human the "right of choice" and as GOD, HE cannot violate HIS own LAW. The multiple millions or perhaps even billions living on earth at this time *MUST* be given the right to choose. And choose is exactly what they do, some to follow Satan in rebellion and the rest to follow GOD into ETERNAL life.

Satan gathers I can only describe as malcontents, an army, according to scripture, as the sand of the sea, and marches to and surrounds "the camp of the saints and the beloved city" (Jerusalem). As with the previous army, this army is also destroyed with a word. Satan is thrown into the "Lake of Fire" where the anti-Christ and the false prophet already reside in torment.

Next is the White Throne Judgment. ALL the dead, unbelievers, will stand before the throne, A WHITE THRONE, and be judged, from the least to the greatest. White is and was throughout the Bible the symbol of purity. They will be judged from a book which is the book of life and books which are the deeds of those standing before Jesus. MY first thoughts were there is a degree of punishment involved. If the name of the individual is NOT found in the Book of Life, then punishment is determined by the deeds in the other books. Then, I realized that it was NOT for a degree of punishment because ALL were thrown into the "Lake of Fire". "The books were opened", to disclose, to each one, the REASON why they were being thrown into "The Lake of Fire". The "books" contain all the past sins and transgressions which were NOT forgiven because of the rejection of JESUS and HIS sacrifice for those sins. Those standing before the ultimate judge come from everywhere and DEATH and Hades, the abode of the souls awaiting judgment, are thrown into the "Lake of Fire".

To let my imagination run wild for a moment; I can almost visualize, someone, suddenly standing among a multitude of people. As the person looks around to see all nationalities of the world and people of all the different races, black, white, brown,yellow and even red. Many are in strange-appearing, at least to that person, clothing until it is realized they are dressed in the attire of ages past. All are standing quiet; no one is talking or making any kind of noise. A man appears on a white throne, wearing a very bright and white robe carrying a large book; others follow carrying stacks of books. People begin to file past the throne. The man looks at the person, runs his fingers up and down or across the pages, shake his head and points for the individual to proceed to his left. Those with the stacks of books flip through the pages and then indicate the person is to go an area to be thrown into the Lake of Fire. The man in the white robe speaks to each one and regardless of the nationality; the person understands exactly what is said. The person watches as each one is judged, first if their name is written in the Book of Life, from the one the man is holding and then out of the books of deeds the others have.

Finally, anyone not found written in the BOOK of LIFE is thrown into the Lake of Fire. This is the reason my writing this document, those thrown into the Lake of Fire are to be forever tormented and in pain. The last words they will hear is: "Depart from me I never knew YOU." These are saddest words ever spoken. What extremely sad words to be spoken from the one, who gave HIS life so those very words would *NOT* HAVE to be said. How sad it will be for the ones that hear these FINAL words, it will be "THE FINAL FAREWELL".

EQUAL

EQUALS SIMPLY MEANS BY ACCEPTING THE SAVING **GRACE** FREELY GIVEN TO EVERYONE by GOD the FATHER, the sacrifice of JESUS HIS SON, the "final farewell" will NOT be heard. GOD does NOT wish any to perish, to be separated from HIS Love and care.

To accept the sacrifice of the SON of GOD for the dissolution of all your sins, past, present and future, it is a simple process; many believe it to be so simple that it cannot be the way. Believe with your heart, Jesus the SON of GOD, came to this world in the form of a man, was condemned, killed by hanging on a cross, was buried and rose from the dead on the third day to sit at the right hand of the Father.

Therefore, "The Final Farewell" will not be heard but replaced by "WEL-COME" into the place prepared for those who LOVE and are LOVED by Jesus and HIS HOLY Angels. This place IS called NEW JERUSALEM; it will be in a NEW HEAVEN where there is PEACE and life will be a pleasure, no tears, pain or heartaches EVER and forever.

ETERNITY

THE FINAL TWO CHAPTERS OF THE BOOK OF REVELATION DESCRIBE THE BEAUTY of the New Heaven and New Jerusalem, the pleasures that await all believers.

New Jerusalem is described as city coming down from heaven, bright as a costly stone, "crystal clear jasper" with a high wall, twelve gates each made from a single pearl, with an angel at each gate. Each gate had the name of a tribe of Israel and each three gates faced a different direction. The city was supported with twelve foundations, each adorned with a different precious gem and with a name of one of the apostles of Jesus on each. The city itself is fifteen HUNDRED MILES long, wide and high. The material makeup of the wall, two hundred sixteen feet high, is jasper and the city is made of pure gold, so pure it is as clear as glass.

There is a river, clear as crystal, coming from the very throne of GOD. On both sides of the river is the TREE of LIFE which will bear twelve different kinds of fruit continuously. The leaves are for the healing of the nations.

All will see the face of Jesus and HIS name will be on their foreheads; there will no longer be any night nor need of any light as the glory of LORD GOD will be their light. WE are the children of "light".

It does not even mention the NEW bodies, which will NEVER wear out, perfect weather conditions ALL the time, perfect health, no illness or disease and I cannot say it enough, be forever with JESUS and our loved ones. The peace and contentment, free from worries and concerns that plague us every day here in this world.

Also, IN MY OPINION, the ability to move about anywhere at the speed of thought, no need to partake of food or water UNLESS we so desire and finally move through solid substances at will. These will be only MINOR perks of the NEW HEAVEN.

For those who may wonder, where is this NEW HEAVEN going to be located? In my opinion, because there is a new earth, with no seas, the NEW HEAVEN will be on the earth and encompass the entire earth.

Add to all this there will be freedom from all the turmoil, pain, heartaches and agony of this world, and be forever in the presence of all the loved ones that preceded us and forever in the presence of JESUS MY LORD!

Does not this sound like a better way to spend an eternity? The choice, as always, is left to the individual. I cannot make it; I can only tell the alternatives. Only one person can make the choice. GOD gave it to every individual. GOD will not force it, only provide the incentive for change.

That is the equation; acceptance minus final farewell equals eternal life. I have presented the equation and the parts of the equation, what is and the reason for "the final farewell" for consideration, to accept or reject is totally up to as the individual. GOD gave everyone the right of choice.

I cannot make it, friends cannot make it, a preacher cannot make it, not even a church membership can make it; the choice is totally and completely up to EACH individual. The ultimate choice was, is and will be eternal LIFE or eternal DEATH.